BEGINNING IN TRIUMPH

To
Nancy
Library
colleague,
Enjoy!
J. Steele

14 June 94

Beginning
in
Triumph

Edith Mucke

Edith Mucke

NORTH STAR PRESS OF ST. CLOUD, INC.

Credits:
An early version of "The Store" was published in *The Plains-woman*, Grand Forks, North Dakota, October 1985.
An early version of "Ironing" was published in *Hurricane Alice*, University of Minnesota English Department, Minneapolis, Minnesota, Vol. 3, No. 4, Fall 1986.

Library of Congress Cataloging-in-Publication Data

Mucke, Edith, 1914-
    Beginning in Triumph   /   Edith Mucke.
    160 p. 21½ cm.
    ISBN: 0-87839-086-3 : $12.95
    1. Mucke, Edith, 1914- —Childhood and youth.   2.
Triumph (Minn.)—Social life and customs.   3. Triumph
(Minn.)—Biography.   4. City and town life—Minnesota—
Triumph.   I. Title.
F614.T48M83   1994   94-15569
977.6′232—dc20   CIP

Printed in the United States of America by Versa Press, Inc., East Peoria, Illinois.

Published by North Star Press of St. Cloud, Inc., P.O. Box 451, St. Cloud, Minnesota 56302.

ISBN: 0-87839-086-3

To be alive — is Power —
Existence — in itself —
Without a further function —
Omnipotence — Enough —

To be alive — and Will!
'Tis able as a God —
The Maker — of Ourselves — be what —
Such being — Finitude!

Emily Dickinson

This book is dedicated to the memory of my husband,
Paul Mucke (1903-1990),

my parents —
Bessie Nelson Johnson (1887-1951)
Alfred Svente Johnson (1879-1952),

for my daughters, Catherine Elizabeth and Jane Lynn

and, of course,
for the children —
all the children.

Acknowledgments

I would like to thank two editors: Mary Rockcastle, writing teacher at the University of Minnesota, whose patience and encouragement got me started and kept me going on the first draft of this material; Corinne A. Dwyer of North Star Press, whose judicious selection and wisdom in the organization of my material created an artful whole and whose response to my words brings me joy unlimited.

I am grateful to authors Paulette Bates Alden and Susan Allen Toth and to the many friends who read early versions and continued to have faith in the meaning of my work.

The Universe
is made up of stories,
not of atoms.

Muriel Rukeyser

Preface

Must I have a reason to tell my story? A need to describe the experiences that caused these typewriter keys to fly? For the love of life's fire within me . . . for the child who lives forever within me . . .

From a shoebox on a shelf high in my closet, I lift a yellowed photograph, a formal family setting taken by Papa's good friend Ernest Krook from Sweden. The photograph shows the vine-covered screened porch of the Little House, but my eyes seek first the face of my beloved mother. Her expression and life were serious, yet a peace glows in her luminous dark eyes, deepset below black brows. She has high cheek bones, but rounded cheeks. A full mouth, closed to cover teeth not quite straight. Her hair, parted on the side sweeps over her left eye in a wave, then lifts back softly over her ears.

In the corner of the porch in the photograph, next to the chair where Mother sits, a plant stand displays a lush Boston fern. Mother's right arm rests lightly on the stand, her fingers drooping gracefully, her sheer Georgette sleeve forming a graceful loop below her wrist. Her left hand rests quietly on

Our family on the front porch of the Little House.

her lap in waves and swirls of dark silk. Above, a low-necked ruffle bunches into froth.

In a child's wicker rocking chair at my mother's knee sits Baby Ruth, perhaps two years old. Her chubby feet in high-buttoned, dark shoes stick straight out in front of her; her small hands stiffly clasped in her lap. Her white dress is heavy with embroidery and ruffles. Her round eyes, dark like Mother's, look out at me from under Buster Brown bangs.

To the left of my Mother, between my parents, I stand. Black patent leather Mary Jane sandals, white stockings, a similar beruffled and embroidered white dress with puffed sleeves and a wide ribbon sash cinched well below my waist-line. Serious expression and Buster Brown haircut.

Mama sits in a straight-backed chair. The large mahogany rocker with back and seat of dark leather and ball-and-claw feet has been moved onto the porch for my father. He wears a black suit. His arms rest on the wide, shiny arms of the chair, his right supporting my formally posed hand.

At the end of his crossed legs, his shoes shine. His coat flares open just enough to display a heavy watch chain draped across his chest. A wide tie and winged collar bind the base of his neck. I admire his beautiful oval head with small ears and dark hair, side parted and very slick. Rimless spectacles frame clear eyes and rest on his fine straight nose. A bushy mustache darkens a pleasant, full mouth. Of the four faces, only his betrays any sign of amusement.

The main street of Triumph.

The main street of Monterey.

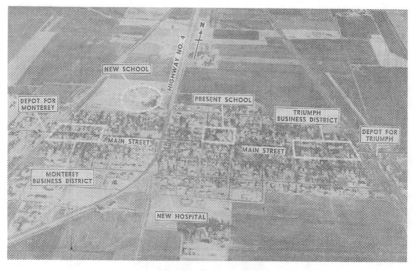

Aerial view of the two towns.

Contents

Part I

1.

White Satin
Wedding Shoes

Yellow with age, white satin wedding shoes. My mother's. I hold the smooth satin to my cheek. Fit my hand into the pointed toe and touch the satin rosette.

The last time I cleaned my basement, fifteen or eighteen years ago, I threw away my own white wedding pumps. I cannot throw away my mother's. Yet I'm trying to simplify my life, one of the demands of growing old.

Order. Lack of clutter. What is a life but a clutter of experiences, of impressions, of memories? I don't like the word "clutter." Confluence. Eudora Welty's word. Coming together. Order out of chaos.

White satin wedding shoes. My mother's white satin wedding shoes. The beginning . . . my beginning . . .

*　　*　　*

A young Swede in a smooth black overcoat stood on a corner waiting for a yellow streetcar. Christmas Eve. Alfred Svente Johnson was a long way from what he still thought of as home. Standing alone in the white and still, he thought of faraway Malmö, Sweden. He thought of his dead mother, his long trip across the Atlantic Ocean, his arrival at the

Duluth seaport where distant relatives had welcomed him
with the best they had, a supper of American weiners and
mashed potatoes. He thought of how well he had mastered
the language, his time in the bookkeeping school, his work
for the Yellow Cab Company and his present work with the
Brin Glass Company. He fingered his well-groomed, brown
mustache, wiped his gold, rimless spectacles, and allowed
himself to feel gratitude for the Christmas Eve invitation
that would overcome his inner emptiness.

A week earlier, Hans, who shared a desk in their large
office at Brin Glass, had invited him to spend Christmas Eve
with him and his family. Hans had not shown up for work
the day before. But Alfred had once before taken the streetcar to Hans' duplex in south Minneapolis. He knew the way.
Hans' wife had served a pot roast Sunday dinner at noon,
and they had spent the afternoon playing cards with the
children, talking, smoking and sipping schnapps. His gratitude swelled.

The streetcar stopped for him, and he climbed aboard.
As he rode, he thought with pleasure of the lutefisk and
boiled potatoes that were sure to be on the table to celebrate this hallowed *julafton*. But when he arrived and walked
up the front steps of the duplex, he saw a sign:

QUARANTINE
SCARLET FEVER

"Poor Hans!" Alfred thought. "How sad to have someone ill and be quarantined for Christmas! He'd probably
been too distracted to remember his invitation to me, or,
perhaps, they didn't have a telephone."

Hans had not forgotten the invitation. A young married
couple, Ella and Oscar Westerdahl, who lived upstairs, were
good friends. With Swedish hospitality, they offered to
watch for the young bookkeeper and to include him in their
own Christmas Eve celebration. Bessie, my mother and Ella's
sister, also was spending Christmas Eve with the Westerdahls.
So when Alfred accepted that Swedish hospitality, he was
introduced to Bessie. And that's how my mother met my
father and how I, much later, happened to be in my basement unable to discard a pair of white satin wedding shoes.

Papa—Alfred Svente Johnson.

Aunt Anna told my sister and me that two suitors were unable to win my mother's hand and that this coming together of Bessie and Alfred was something like love at first sight. Unwilling to spend much time or energy looking backward, my mother rarely talked of the glamour of Alfred's courtship. But Aunt Anna reported that Alfred impressed everyone—"a true aristocrat" she called him, always stylishly dressed. ("He sometimes carried a cane with gold engraved handles." It, too, rests in my basement.) Alfred took Bessie to the best restaurants.

Papa was no youngster at the time he met my mother, probably thirty-two. A photograph taken in Sweden portrays his perfectly oval face, clear eyes behind rimless glasses, and his straight nose just short of Roman—a fine classical nose. The merest suggestion of a cleft in the chin gives him a noble face, I think. In a wide-lapeled, dark suitcoat, a white shirt with stiff-winged collar and a wide, flowing cravat, his straight shoulders give the effect of a strong person in a slim body. His expression seems serious, thoughtful, with perhaps

Mother—Bessie Nelson Johnson.

just a suggestion of disdain. Or do I see that because the Papa I knew was proud and often felt himself to be superior?

A photograph of Bessie taken in Moline shows a lovely lady standing erect in front of heavy, tasseled draperies. The look in her eyes is one I know well, as though, fully aware of "the tragic human condition," she looks with compassion, tenderness and caring upon the world.

Their courtship included Sunday trolley car trips to Lake Harriet for picnics and band concerts. I wish I knew more. My favorite story is "The Night Papa Gave Mother Her Diamond Engagement Ring."

Riding the streetcar from St. Louis Park, Bessie and Alfred went to Schieks Cafe in downtown Minneapolis where, in rich and quiet light, liveried waiters served them an elegant dinner on white tablecloths. They went on to the Metropolitan Theatre where they saw "The Pink Lady" opera. And then, on the yellow streetcar clanging on metal tracks through the dark night, they rode out to St. Louis

Park. There, across the tracks from the grey-timbered waiting station at the end of the line, Papa gave Mama the gold engagement ring. A diamond standing high on its delicate prongs shone under the tall street lights.

I said that Papa's expression in that early photograph is serious and that he was not young. Certainly, he was not impetuous. Papa had some problem with one knee, and, before they were married, he wanted it treated. And, since Papa believed that everything and every service was better in Sweden than in this country, he sailed off to Sweden for knee surgery. Perhaps he simply needed a reason to make a return trip to his homeland, to take another look at the southern tip of Sweden, the Swedish Riviera, where he dreamed of one day owning a summer or retirement home. I can't think he needed extra time to think things over because, besides the diamond ring, he had bought Bessie a New Home sewing machine. While he was gone, she worked on her trousseau and her hope chest. I can imagine her making tiny stitches in stiff linen napkins (some of which I still iron), embroidering "J" in satin stitch in the corners of those napkins, fashioning pillow cases and hemming sheets. Oh, she could make the treadle of that machine fly.

Tinted photographs taken some time after the marriage reveal two faces somewhat fuller. Papa's hair parts in the middle; mother does not wear a hat. In her pink lace dress, her curly brown hair piled high and wearing the ruby-studded gold bracelet with the difficult clasp that my daughter Jane now wears, my mother looks elegant indeed. Papa's cravat is even larger than before, and his face carries a very serious expression.

Papa was thirty-four and Mother twenty-six when they married. In one of my cluttered upstairs drawers lies a rolled certificate of marriage inscribed in Swedish and signed by Carl Peterson, Lutheran Pastor. Green leaves, roses and doves border its edges. At the bottom is a dramatic rendering of an open Bible and, at the top, two people walking hand in hand on a pink path in a pink, red and green garden toward a white sun whose five wide rays reach upward toward heaven. This elaborate, though yellowed, document marks their August 30, 1913, wedding.

*   *   *

In 1914 the Archduke of Austria was murdered. On Flag Day, the 14th of June, I was born. The yellowed satin wedding shoes are still in my basement.

There are some enterprises in which
a careful disorderliness is the
true method.

Herman Melville

2.

Thin Edge of
the Wedge

Underneath a table, while still talking baby talk, James Joyce heard adult conversation. Modern poets write hauntingly of sensations while in the uterus. Psychiatrists ask, "What is your first memory?"

My earliest memory is of peeling the protective covering of a newly planted sapling. I remember how it felt—smooth, slippery, glossy, polished. The pale yellow-green satin slid off so deliciously. I do not remember being caught in the act; I remember only that when my father came home he was supposed to spank me. I see my mother standing in the doorway of the small bedroom that held her New Home sewing machine. The room had a large window that looked out on the screened front porch. The punishment must have been mild, for I have no memory of pain.

In my second memory, I was little, close to the floor, sitting on a china potty. I was crying. I did not want Mormor, my grandmother, to wipe my bottom because her hands were wrinkled and rough—not gentle, not smooth like Mama's.

And another: Mama had a highly decorated silver dresser set—comb, brush, mirror, and two little silver boxes. One box had a cover with a hole in it for hair she cleaned from her brush and comb. I slid the point of a pin over the silver back of the mirror. Smoothly, silently, the pin moved. No memory of punishment, only an "X" that would never go away no matter how much my hands wiped and polished.

* * *

I have no memories of the house in which I was born, 2409 Chicago Avenue in Minneapolis. The sapling whose tender bark I removed was planted by the owner of a house my parents rented on Brunswick Avenue in St. Louis Park shortly after I was born. A light brown bungalow with two bedrooms and a large front porch, we always called it the Little House. My sister Ruth was born there.

When we lived in the Little House, my mother's parents (Mor and For) lived in a nearby two-story frame house painted a dull battleship grey. Walking to Mormor's house meant going north past the block of the Park (where our grandfather mowed the grass and we went to ice cream socials), across the railroad tracks past the Emmen Saint L depot, through Farmer Seirup's cornfields, where the corn always seemed high, and past two more blocks of frame houses, all painted grey by memory, to the big house on the hill.

My early Christmases . . . the images blur. *Julafton* (Christmas Eve) afternoon Ruth and I were bundled up and taken to Mormor's house, while our parents attended to other business. Mormor bustled about all afternoon. Baby Ruth napped while For sang Swedish songs and rode me horseback on his knee.

When Papa and Mama returned, we all sat down at the round oak table laid with white muslin cloth and plain white dishes. The traditional Christmas Eve meal started with *sylta* (head cheese) and red pickled beets served with plain boiled potatoes; then more white boiled potatoes, mustard gravy and steaming platters of lutefisk; last of all, *risgrynsgröt* (rice pudding) with an almond in it. The person who found the almond in his or her bowl was to be married first.

After supper, with Papa carrying Ruthie, we walked home through the cold, white night. While we were gone, something wonderful had happened. In the middle of the plain living room stood a tall green Christmas tree! Red cloth Santas with long white beards, shiny colored balls, chains of silver tinsel, and even tiny colored birds hung from the branches. And clipped to the ends of the branches in their metal holders were tiny wax candles.

Following exclamations and explanations that Santa had been there, came a quiet time while Mama and Papa struck matches and lighted the slim candles. What a sight! All the splendor. But more. Presents under the tree. I have only a vague memory of opening presents when very young but a vivid image of a big doll named Betty with real blonde hair and brown eyes that opened and closed.

*   *   *

Two blocks east of us stood Frieland's Grocery, a small store I remember best for its penny candy and long, twisted strips of black licorice. Mama sent me there alone one day to buy a cake of Fleischman's yeast. Unable to resist the shiny foil wrapping, I nibbled at the edges while walking home, until a cat started to follow me, and I came home crying because I didn't like the cat.

Next door to us lived the Dickinson family—Dick and Nora with their two children, Bruce and Evelyn. Irish Nora, good-humored and laughing, embraced the world. She loved crossword puzzles, Shakespeare, newspapers, Abe Lincoln, politics, and clean curtains. She delighted in movies and Rudolph Valentino, birdsong early in the morning, and making doughnuts for neighborhood children as well as her own. Mrs. "Dick" always came up with schemes to make money. Somewhere, not as far away as over the rainbow, she knew a fortune waited for her family.

While husband Dick went off to Texas to buy and sell land (and bring back the first grapefruit Ruth and I ever tasted), Nora managed everything at home. And she knew how to manage. No ends of soap bars ever were tossed aside (a small cake of Ivory lived in a steel basket to be whisked about in the dishpan before washing the dishes); bits of cracklings were added to fried potatoes; crusts of bread asked only for a few raisins to make a fine pudding. No one drank or smoked in that house. To this day the memory of her house carries special smells, of sheets dried in the sun, naptha soap, and furniture polish bearing no relationship to the odor of Mr. Clean or Pledge or pine.

Mr. Dick claimed the noted Emily of Amhurst as an ancestor. A tall man with flat face, pale hair and broad smile, he shuffled along, calm and gentle, agreeing with Nora and his mother-in-law, Gramma Duff. His wisecracking mixed well with Nora's Irish wit and made for a repartee that contrasted sharply with the serious conversations of my own parents. Dick and Nora played cribbage together in the evenings; my parents read.

Five years older than I, Bruce Dickinson, a lank, freckle-faced kid, would have nothing to do with his sister Evelyn, Ruth or me. Evelyn, in age between Ruth and me, had a long face and hair as straight as a board. Nora and my mother became good friends. They stitched identical black sateen dresses and bloomers for the three of us. And we played together—in the sandbox, on the big lawns, on the screened porches.

Sometimes we fought, but the battles broke along well-defined lines. When, one sunny morning two of us stuck out our tongues at the third black-costumed child, I looked quickly at the person across from me and then at the person beside me. I was on the wrong side. I ran quickly to the other side of the porch and stuck my tongue out at Evelyn. Ruth and I were sisters. We belonged together. But when Marjorie Christianson, who lived one block west of us, wanted to join in our play, we said no. She insisted and cried. We told her to go get her doll. She did. But when she came into the yard, the three of us, side by side, threw pebbles at her until she ran home crying.

Alliances changed when I started first grade. Walking the two blocks to the school across from Frieland's Grocery made me feel important. One day when I came out for recess with the rest of the first graders, I found Evelyn and Ruth playing on the school swings. With great authority I sent them home. They were not old enough to go to school and must not play on *my* swings!

Gramma Duff, Nora's mother, lived next door to the Dickinsons. She had lived in Mille Lacs, supporting herself by running the one hotel in that northern Minnesota town. When Nora married, her mother sold the hotel and, with the profits, built two identical frame houses side by side on Brunswick Avenue. She had them constructed so that the two porches and back steps faced each other. I remember that Evelyn, Ruth and I played dolls on those two back porches. Evelyn had the largest doll, Gertrude, with real flaxen hair long enough to brush and braid. She also had a black doll. I remember one time when Ruth, who crawled longer than most children, even after she learned to walk, crawled from our back steps to the Duff-Dickinson steps, dragging the black doll with her.

While Nora and Dick lived in one house and had their babies, Gramma Duff lived in the other and kept roomers. Pale faced, her white hair piled high, with a firmly corseted figure and straight back, Gramma Duff was an imposing figure. She usually dressed in black. Though a staunch Catholic, she was such a strong woman that she allowed herself the freedom to disagree with the priest when she found it more practical. In the two houses, her word was law. She was a second grandmother to Ruth and me. I loved and feared her.

During those early years with Evelyn as my friend, Mrs. Dick was always there, ministering to our needs, guiding and watching. Both her children had well-stocked bookcases in their bedrooms. And her love of crosswords made her word conscious, so that we had our vocabularies enriched and even played spelling games. Mrs. Dick loved cards and games and taught Ruthie and me to play old maid, pounce, rummy, many forms of solitaire, and even fifty-two pick up.

And how she fed us! In the large breakfast nook with the wide and sturdy oak benches and the oilcloth-covered table, we ate peanut butter and jelly sandwiches on home-baked bread, "Dutch Cake" topped with sour cream and cinnamon, thick molasses cookies washed down with tall glasses of milk cooled by a block of ice in the brown wooden icebox. Sometimes we had contests to see who could eat the most sweet corn. Bruce always won.

Yes, Bruce was part of our play. Having neither brothers nor boy cousins our own age, Ruth and I knew our first male playmate at the Dickinson house. Skinny, freckle-faced Bruce had red hair, a long thin nose over thin lips and a great roaring laugh. A talented piano player, he spent a lot of time with his "nose in a book" (like me) and, although he never new it, he was my first love.

* * *

Of the Little House, I remember best the kitchen. With windows between dark cupboards, the Majestic electric stove standing high on its metal legs, this large room had linoleum designed to look like bricks. Black lines deeper than the various shades of red brick made ridges in the floor. On her hands and knees, Mama scrubbed it with a stiff brush and then covered it with newspapers for half a day. In the corner of the room, the corner near the broom closet with the narrow, varnished brown-yellow door, was the hot air register where I stood on cold winter mornings warming myself and my scratchy, long-legged winter underwear with the drop seat before I put my skinny legs into it. The underwear was never as tight at the bottom as I wanted, and I folded the cuffs over, making ugly lumps under my black stockings.

* * *

I have a vivid memory of the day I learned that Papa had bought the store in Triumph and that we were to move— away from Evelyn. Away from Mormor. I said I wouldn't go. I didn't want to leave St. Louis Park, my friends and my school. I cried and cried. I remember my legs flying, hitting the green grass and then hard earth and sidewalks. I ran and ran . . . and cried . . .

3.

The Store

"If I had known when I first came to Triumph that I would spend thirty years of my life here," my mother said, "I'd have lain right down on the spot and died."

Papa bought the store the year I was seven years old. It stood on the main street of Triumph, Minnesota. On the west side of the two-story frame building where the sun shone brightly every afternoon, in large letters, carefully painted in green and black on a beige background, the sign read:

ALFRED S. JOHNSON
GENERAL MERCHANDISE
GROCERIES — DRY GOODS — MEATS — SHOES
WE SATISFY

I have tried to imagine what it was like for Mother. "Herre gud!" she might have exclaimed. "This town! No paved streets, not even electric lights."

As a child in Sweden, where no electricity existed, she knew life was possible without that energy, but since then she had lived in American cities—Moline, Illinois, and Minneapolis, Minnesota—where people had electric stoves as well as electric lights. And, instead of a house in Triumph, we

The store in Triumph, Minnesota.

lived upstairs over the store. True, Mother and Father owned the store, but not having a real house with a basement must have been hard for her. But mother enjoyed having her sister nearby. Ella and her husband, Oscar, owned a hardware store in the neighboring town of Monterey, separated from Triumph only by a road that bisected Main street, a road whose southern extremity ended in a corn field and whose northern limit viewed wheat fields.

Papa, Mama, Ruth and I arrived in July, moving all the household furniture and possessions into the upper story of the flat-topped building on which the sun so mercilessly beat. The old walnut chiffonaire that Papa had brought from Sweden came, along with the brass bed, the mahogany dressing table with the swinging oval mirror, the round Mission oak dining table and chairs with brown leather-covered seats, and the heavy mahogany living room chairs—one straight and one the rocker on which Ruthie one day rocked too hard, swung too far, and crushed her thumb as she and the rocker both went over. And with us also were the Swedish linens and those napkins with the letter "J" that I still use and love to iron.

Hot. How hot it was that July! So hot, my mother said, that Ruth and I refused to go outside to play. Strangers in a new place, afraid to go outside because someone might talk to us—or maybe no one would talk to us—we lay on the floor in our little white vests and the black sateen bloomers that matched the black sateen dresses mother and Nora Dickinson had made for us and Evelyn. Outside a southern breeze—not cool, but a breeze—developed, and the grass-covered corner lot next to the store was open. How Mama must have wished we would go outdoors and leave her alone to settle.

I imagine she wondered what life in Triumph would be like for her children. Surely one day the family would move back to Minneapolis!

In 1921 only four hundred people lived in Triumph and three hundred in Monterey. But Mama knew her husband was excited and happy—like a child in his enthusiasm. America was really the promised land. No longer would Alfred have to take a streetcar downtown every morning, riding the long way to the Brin Glass Company. Not that Brin hadn't been good to Alfred. But Mama guessed that every man's dream was to be his own boss. The books Papa kept would be *his* books, recording *his* money to pay *his* debts.

But the dust. How much dust Mama saw rising from Main Street. So easily moved by the strong prairie winds, this dust would show up on her window sills, sifting through doors and windows onto her furniture. Living right on Main Street in a town that didn't even have a gas station! (Years later, when Standard Oil built a station that my mother could see from the living room and kitchen windows, she would rejoice. Civilization had arrived.) But Ella in Monterey would keep her from being lonesome, and the Triumph Embroidery Club would welcome her as a member.

No Christian Science Church. Mother missed that and her friend and neighbor, Nora Dickinson, who had introduced her to that beautiful religion. Baptized and confirmed in the Lutheran church, Mama always had had a strong faith in the existence of God, but explaining all the troubles and sorrow of life gave her pause. What a blessed relief for this optimistic Bessie to substitute the joy and hope of Christian Science for the dour, gloomy Lutheranism—all that fire and damnation. Daily, she opened her Bible and *Science and Health with Key to the Scriptures* by Mary Baker Eddy and, using her worn dictionary when necessary, studied the lesson for the week. All would be well—all *was* well. On her kitchen wall hung a small brown plaque:

> This is God's spiritual household. No thought can enter which can disturb or annoy any of its members or cause them to manifest sin, disease, or discouragement, for God Good alone governs this household with Perfect Peace and Love and governs every member of it.

The print was dark brown and the capitals red. This "Truth" blazing in her head and heart would help her maintain harmony in the Triumph household above the store.

Anyway, she did not expect that they would be in that Godforsaken place for long. Alfred thought chances were that a good living and a Big Future could be had in Triumph. But the family would not stay in Triumph forever. When we gave Mama Christmas or birthday presents for which she could not quite find use, she would say, "I'll save this until we move back to Minneapolis."

Yes, "Herre gud!" she may have exclaimed, but she settled in.

*   *   *

At the far west end of the two villages stood the Milwaukee and St. Louis depot with its parallel, shining steel tracks leading north and south. The Chicago Northwestern Railroad marked the east end of the two villages. Tracks . . . time and space. From a bakery in Estherville, Iowa, the "Em 'n' St. L" brought wobbly wooden crates filled with warm loaves of bread—pound loaves, pound and a half loaves, mostly white, some half white and half whole wheat, a few of rye— all soft and wrapped in heavy red, white and blue waxed paper. A horse-drawn wagon delivered the flimsy crates to the store. My mother, unwilling to settle for this stuff with the consistency of marshmallows, baked her own golden loaves—caraway rye, and three-day buns (a Triumph Embroidery Club recipe).

The two little villages were bordered east and west by the double lines of the railroad tracks. My parents, Aunt Ella, and Uncle Oscar predicted that when Mayor Schwalen of Triumph and Mayor Peterson of Monterey died, the two villages would become one town. Then, instead of having a village with four hundred inhabitants and another with three hundred, a real *town* with a population of seven hundred people would exist. They were right. Years later a letter I addressed to Triumph, Minnesota, came back to me marked "No Such Town." The villages had become one, Trimont.

In the corner lot, vacant and high with weeds, that came with the store, Ruth and I played "house" in rooms that had rugs for floors, blankets for ceilings, and high weeds for walls. Later, Papa cut the weeds, cultivated and planted a garden, sowed grass and planted trees. On summer evenings kids from all over town gathered for games of hide and seek, run-sheep-run, kick-the-can, and, later, croquet. On summer mornings Ruth and I cleaned radishes and onions in the garden, strung bead necklaces and polished our finger nails, read *Dandelion Cottage* and *Elsie Dinsmore*, planned weiner roasts and connived strategies with our friends to get our mothers to say yes to movies or dates. Eventually, up-to-date lawn furniture was added, becoming the stage for countless Brownie camera shots.

*   *   *

Papa knew nothing about merchandising, but in 1921 that didn't prevent his success. Papa made money. Electricity came to town. Electric lights replaced kerosene lamps and gas lights with their fragile mantles. A "fridge" replaced the ice box. Papa took Mother to Minneapolis on a no-holds-barred buying trip. A black sealskin fur coat for Mother. Upholstered mohair davenport and chairs. Wilton rugs. A walnut Jacobean dining room set complete with china closet, buffet, and even a clock that marked the quarter hours with Westminster chimes. This set replaced the mahogany and leather chairs and the Mission oak dining room furniture that had come with us from Minneapolis. Mother made black and gold damask draperies for the dining and living room windows. Ruth and I were always proud to bring our friends to that home above the store.

Martha Peterson came with the store. She had worked for the two previous owners and was with us until Papa sold the store. Martha, twenty-seven years old when we bought the store in 1921, remained a loyal servant, a true friend, and a great supporter of our family. "Faithful Old Retainer" Ruth and I used to call her; in truth, she "retained" us as much or more than we did her. Following the 1929 stock market crash when Papa lost more than enough money to send Ruth and me to college and the creditors were on his neck and we could only buy merchandise C.O.D., Martha loaned Papa money. Even long after those years, when we were in our sixties, Ruth and I kept in touch with Martha, heard from her at Christmas and on our birthdays, and remembered her with cards and letters.

Other help in the store included Ida, Doc, the King, and a succession of young boys who unloaded boxes, unpacked groceries, and swept the oily reddish brown sweeping compound from the narrow-planked, hardwood floor.

The King, a tall, lanky Swede with bushy hair and a fondness for vanilla and almond extract—Prohibition favorites—did odd jobs around the place, figuring in my memory mostly for his contribution to long and irrepressible fits of laughter for my sister and me. He prided himself on a vocabulary of polysyllabic words. Carrying in sacks of salt that had become very hard, he said, "After I pile these up on this shelf, I shall masticate them to soften them."

The King lived in a small green house half a block from the store. But for the fresh paint and the neatness, it would have been a shack. Often Sunday noons, just before we sat down to our chicken or pot roast dinner, Ruth and I would be sent over to the King's house with a generous portion of steaming hot food—mashed potatoes and gravy included— and mother's homemade biscuits. I know nothing of the King's origins or what finally happened to him. I know that my father loved and respected him for his native intelligence, inherent good manners, and industry. Father grieved over his spasmodic bouts of drunkenness.

Doc, our jovial, round butcher, made "Johnson's Home Made Weiners" and Swedish sausage in the red brick smoke house my father built. Doc had curved, rounded hands, his fingers as plump and hard as the sausages he made. He wore a blood-stained apron when he hauled in gory sides of beef. Doc smoked hams and bacon for our market and also for farmers, joking with everyone who came into the store. He kept the sawdust on his floor space white and clean, sharpened the lethal knives, and fussed when too many foodstuffs took over a part of his big cooler. On hot summer days Ruth and I pleaded to be allowed to stand in that cooler.

Doc had no family, and his great expertise outside of butchering was card playing. All-night card games, mostly poker, were common inside the grimy windows of Dettmer's Pool Room and Billiard Parlor on Main Street.

Ida, large boned and good natured with blue bubble eyes, also worked at the store. During dull hours waiting for customers who never came or straggled in evenings and at the end of the day, Ida finished a high school correspondence course. She liked to sing, but Ruth and I giggled at her high-pitched voice.

The store kept long hours. I remember hearing Pete Frahm's hearty voice booming, "Good Morning!" to Papa before I was out of bed on a summer morning. Pete owned the furniture store across the street, and his family, like ours, lived upstairs over their store.

On Wednesday and Saturday nights the store came alive. All the farmers came to town, bringing crates of eggs and crocks of butter churned by their wives to trade for groceries. They bought their weekly supplies of staples— cans of peas and corn, boxes of Jell-O in raspberry, strawberry, lemon and orange flavors, one-hundred-pound sacks of flour, ten- and twenty-five-pound bags of salt and sugar. Sometimes midnight arrived before all the farmers returned from the pool halls to pick up their wives and children and all their groceries.

But other summer days could be slow. Martha and Ida sat on stools behind the counters, reading church literature, doing their "lessons," stitching "fancy work" on round wooden hoops, or sewing clothes for Ruth's and my dolls. At Christmas we found the results of all those not so idle hours— red wool doll dresses trimmed in satin braid and shiny black buttons and soft white dimity dresses with lace ruffles. During the early years, the good years, mother did not work in the store but devoted her time to Ruthie and me, her housekeeping, her sewing, coffee parties, and the Triumph Embroidery Club. As we grew older, mother "helped out" more and more in the store. I can see her coming wearily up the stairs at midnight on a Saturday. She heated water in the white enamel tea kettle to soak her feet, her calloused feet with a corn on one little toe and a bunion on the left foot.

And when Ruth and I were old enough, we too helped out. With heavy aluminum scoops, we dished out sticky prunes and apricots from wooden boxes into brown paper sacks. Toledo brass scales had fine gradations that I had to step on a box or on tiptoe to read. We pushed the metal plates of the adding machine up or down and moved the lever for the total. Two pounds of prunes, seventeen cents. One pound of apricots, ten cents. Rice and navy beans in sacks: five pounds, three pounds, one. Coffee arrived in one-hundred-pound sacks; we ground each order with the coffee grinder, carefully turning the three-foot wheel. Later we had a fancy electric grinder.

On the dry goods side of the store were large bolts of material—black sateen, various grades of muslin, printed percales and large checked ginghams. We carried pillow tubing, cotton batting for quilts, stamped "fancy work" ready to be embroidered with the grand variety of silk or cotton six-strand floss. A large revolving case held rows and rows of colored thread, numbers 20 and 60, rick-rack, bias tapes in rainbow colors, silver hooks and eyes, black snaps, and buttons—small, medium and large, two-holed and four-holed, pearl and colored. Glass counters supported glass-shelf displays of manicure sets, tortoise-shell dresser sets, embroidered handkerchiefs, fountain pen-and-pencil sets, china cream and sugar sets, glass pickle dishes, perfumes, figurines and small glass animals.

Display windows at the front of the store were always

ammonia clean. Grocery items decorated the east windows—
one week Kellogg's Corn Flakes, Post Bran Flakes, and
Wheaties, Campbell's soups the next week, Atwood's coffee
and Hershey's cocoa during another. In the west window we
draped yards of fabric or displayed men's underwear. I remember a bolt of brown satin over steel standards gathered in
the middle to show how it looked "made up" using one of our
Butterick patterns. Ida made the window arrangements.
Standing on the sidewalk, viewing the display from the outside, I would approve, "Yes, looks good—like Minneapolis."

At Alfred S. Johnson's Store, when someone telephoned
in an order of groceries, we made sure everything on the list
was delivered, even if we had to run to our competitor's
store to get it. And we were fast. Papa delivered groceries in
his little green Pontiac several times a day. Papa was known
to drive to Mrs. Meehan's with Ry Krisp, complaining how
silly she was to buy Ry Krisp because it was slimming, when
she said it was "very good if eaten with lots of butter on it,"
or with a few bars of Fels Naptha soap to pleasant, laughing
Irene Schmidt who gave me Dostoyevsky to read when I was
twelve.

Before the harvest, farmers' bills ran into thousands
of dollars. We posted grocery slips in large black folding
sheets of metal near Papa's desk in the rear of the building.
At the family dinner table we heard comments, sometimes
groans, about the amount of some accounts, but I cannot
remember anyone who was denied credit. During the summer
large families of Mexican migrant beet workers chalked up
debts that were paid before they returned south for the
winter. Experienced accountant that he was, Papa kept
meticulous books, his ledgers filled with his flowery script
and rows of artfully penned numbers in green ink.

The customer was always right. Always. Not only were
Ruth and I brought up in a society in which women were expected to please men, working in the store trained us to please
everyone.

"Herre gud," my beloved mother may have said, but,
thirty years later, when Papa sold the store for cash and returned—"came home"—to Minneapolis, she was ready to
admit that we had had a good life in Triumph.

Sisters, Edith and Ruth, c. 1922.

4.

Summertime

As a child in Triumph, on days when the dusty gravel road flared white hot and waves of heat rose from the yellow wheat fields just outside of town, my sister, Ruth, and I, brown bags hanging from the handlebars, rode our bicycles east of town. Red-faced, often having to stand on the pedals to make the hills, our hands clammy on the black rubber handle bars, we pedaled down the middle of a stony road until we came to a small bridge. Braking, spattering gravel, we left the road, dropped our bicycles on the ground and inched our skinny bodies under barbed wire fences.

Through a pasture and beside the still water of the creek, we walked to the gravel pit, carrying our paper bag lunches. Sitting on the edge, we looked down into what we thought was a bottomless pit, a mysterious black well of icy water. But the water level rested so far below where we sat that we could not dip our hot feet into it. Cool air rose to our sweating faces.

We relished the lunch in our brown paper bags, naming the bread and cheese "manna" and, unscrewing the tops of the glass Mason jars, drank summer-warmed milk. We worshiped simplicity and nature, adamant not to include anyone on those bike expeditions into the country who would desecrate the air by smoking a cigarette. Mysterious the water. Rarefied the atmosphere.

Having done away with the day's manna, we left the gravel pit and allowed our bodies to crumple in the shade of the willow trees—three green-yellow willows, whose weeping branches formed an oasis beside the creek that ran through the flat Martin County farmlands. As the heat flowed out and away from us, we listened to the meadow larks, breathed deeply of the sweet clover and ripening grain and recited poetry.

> It was many and many a year ago,
>   In a kingdom by the sea,
> That a maiden there lived whom you may know
>   By the name of Annabel Lee.
> And this maiden she lived with no other thought
>   Than to love and be loved by me.

Ruth and I took the Red Cross swimming lessons at Johnny Hanson's at Cedar Lake and passed all the fundamental lifesaving examinations, allowing us to spend days alone at the lake. Weathered Johnny Hanson, a farmer with pale blue eyes, hair the color of wet sand and furrows down the sides of his face, allowed Papa to leave the rowboat that he bought for fishing docked at the Hanson farm bordering on Cedar Lake.

Ruth and I had summer friends and winter friends. Gertrude Clute, not in my grade nor in Ruthie's, was our mutual summer friend. She had red hair and large, pale freckles. I was fascinated by her nearly white eyelashes that curled so naturally. Gertrude too had passed the Red Cross tests, and her mother trusted her in the water.

Papa drove Ruth, Gertrude and me to the lake for the day. We swam and learned to dive. My sister, a far more skilled acrobat than I, outshone me in diving. We lay on the raft, lathered our bodies with pale yellow cocoa butter, turned our arms and legs "inside out" to even the tan, and described the pictures we saw in the insides of our closed eyelids. I saw a castle all gold and silver shining. Ruthie saw our German police dog, Reno, running after sheep.

We brought peanut butter and crackers with us and bought cream soda pop from Johnny. Rowing Papa's boat, we took turns swimming the mile or more across the lake. It seemed a long way, and we were proud and happy when we reached the shore.

* * *

Summertime, unlimited freedom, an open landscape.

Our mother's memories of the Baltic Sea, rolling country-side and green hills clouded her appreciation of the mid-western plains country of Martin County. She could not quite forgive the land for its plainness. But Ruthie and I knew that open space as a different place. No neighboring roofs or tall buildings obscured the red circle as it popped up from under the bottom of the eastern sky. We were as free as that sun. Free to run and explore.

One avenue for such adventure was the railroad tracks. At the far east end of Triumph stood the Chicago North-western Railroad depot with its shining steel parallel tracks leading north and south. Those tracks carried the trains, whose romantic whistles I heard in the dark of night and again at high noon.

On the tracks near the depot, Ruth and I picked up thin metal strips with round balls at either end. Great sport consisted of placing these strips on a rail, waiting for a train to come by and then gleefully recovering the flattened objects. We also flattened safety pins and nails.

We took our lunch and walked miles along the tracks. To step from one wooden tie to the next was an absurdly short step, to skip a tie awkwardly long. We climbed across a high trestle to a pasture to feast on peanut butter and jelly sandwiches, apples, cookies and nickel Hershey bars that broke into tiny squares. I sometimes finished my Hershey bar first and tried to convince Ruthie that hers was bigger and she should share.

We pretended to be pioneers in a strange land. We picked up stones or small bottles, a discarded comb, a ring that may have come from a Cracker Jacks box and told our-selves that our finds confirmed the existence of a civilization we were about to discover. Everything we found was a treasure.

One day on those railroad tracks, Ruth and I picked a large bunch of goldenrod for Lura Frahm, our mother's friend with black hair wound about her head in braids. She made raised doughnuts lighter than clouds. When we presented her with our enormous bouquet, she smiled, thanked us kindly and gave us each a frosted chocolate cookie with a pecan on top. We learned later that goldenrod was the evil that set her hay fever rocketing.

*   *   *

Flies buzzed. Invisible cicadas hummed. Under Bergesen's spreading elm, big Hilda, with the large square hands, Ruthie and I made Indian headbands of colored beads. From wooden cigar boxes Papa fashioned looms—linen thread strung through razor-thin slots formed the warp. Closely watching the graph paper patterns we designed, we wove tiny glass beads between taut threads. The silver needles, on which we strung the beads, were long and thin and the holes in the beads hard to see. My fingers grew sticky from concentration and the heat.

Hilda, old enough to babysit Ruth and me, tried to boss us around. We put up with her. Ruth and I shared a secret: we don't like Hilda's bossing, but we liked sharing the shade of *her* tree. Hilda went into her house, returning with dark red Kool Aid for all three of us. I continued to bend my near-sighted eyes over the sauce dish of beads, counting squares in the graph, stringing the beads, pushing them through the warp and pulling the thread tight. Finished, I would have a beaded headband with a red canoe, yellow paddles and white diamond designs on a blue background, proclaiming my chosen Indian name, Nawatasi, meaning, "Be independent. Paddle your own canoe."

Hilda had more than Kool Aid and a shade tree to hold us. Hidden inside a shed in the back of the lot she had *True Confessions* magazines—limp, pages missing, but a delicious break from our craftwork. Leaving our sticky glasses to the flies, we entered the shed. Inside, the dank and dark created

an illusion of coolness. Huddled around the small window
that emitted dusty light, each with her own magazine, we
gobbled up stories of young girls who yielded too easily to
temptation, girls whose love of romance and wealth over-
came their mothers' teachings, young girls who were not
pure or good or true. We read of glamorous young love and
learned that easy riches had a dark side. Girls were left alone
with babies who cried all the time. Life was hard, and wicked-
ness did not go unpunished.

"Listen to this!" Ruthie said and read aloud of another
young girl betrayed by a drunken husband but who rose,
through sorrow and tribulation, to a new life. "But listen
to this . . ." and Hilda read the description of a blonde
dressed in red satin who left her baby to be raised as an
orphan.

We read that "the course of true love never runs smooth,"
and if a girl wanted to get married and live happily ever after,
she'd best be a good girl. We wept over the fate of the poor
heroines and devoured the details of the love affairs.

*   *   *

In our own yard, I sat on a hard white wooden-slat bench,
the heat from my body escaping through the openings between the slats. My bare feet rested in a pail of icy water
pumped from the hardwater well in our back yard. When
the water warmed, I threw it out and pumped a fresh pail.
Sometimes I put my whole head under the spout, gasping
from the blast of cold water. My wet hair kept me cool.

During summers, I read and read. I discovered at the age
of eleven or twelve that the State Library in St. Paul would
mail me a stack of books when I wrote them with requests.
Through *Parnassus on Wheels*, I discovered Christopher
Morley and went on to *The Haunted Bookshop*. I made a
lifelong friend. I read Sherwood Anderson and saw our town
in his language. Ellen Glasgow intrigued me, and I wrote the
State Library for her other books.

Lazy unhurried days. No concern for time.

Ruth and I had time to look at pictures too. In our house
above the store were two large storerooms. Along with trunks

that came from Sweden, winter blankets, a baby crib, heavy brown and red ledgers and a discarded oak buffet that housed Papa's alcoholic beverages, lay stacks of *National Georgraphic* magazines. We invited our friends to see the pictures of unclothed South Sea Islanders and Africans. Little girls without brothers, we stared at the boys' "private parts" and giggled.

Sometimes when Mother was away, we sat on the floor in front of the mahogany bookcase in our parents' bedroom. Behind the three glass doors were leather-bound volumes of books printed in Swedish. Walter Scott's *Ivanhoe, Sagas* with elaborate etchings of Viking gods, our mother's English novels by John Fox, Jr., Mrs. E.D.E.N. Southworth, and Elinor Gynn's *Three Weeks.* Coins from many foreign countries covered a brass tray on a lower shelf. Soon losing interest in these, Ruth and I went for the thick, pale-green *Doctor's Book* that had pictures of a baby curled inside the mother's stomach. Such a big head for the tiny hands and feet. We didn't quite understand.

*   *   *

We welcomed evenings when the merciless sun slid toward the horizon. Ruth and I waited impatiently for Mama and Papa to finish their after-supper coffee. In our first automobile—a black Dodge touring car—we would go for a ride to cool off. In the event of rain, we had side curtains that our parents put up—with grunts or oaths or laughter, depending on the mood. When the evening was hot, we might ride as far as Sherburn and buy ice cream cones.

Papa drove in fits and starts, sometimes cranking the car. We flew at the rapid speed of twenty miles per hour through the main streets of Triumph and Monterey, driving west toward Cedar Lake, then south on the road to Sherburn, over small bridges, across railroad tracks with the black-and-white STOP-LOOK-LISTEN crosses.

In the front seat, our parents commented on the height of the corn or the state of the barley and oats. Ruth and I giggled and were told to be quiet. We pretended we were Lillian Gish and Monte Blue traveling cross country for a mysterious rendezvous. The western skies grew rosy-pink with dusk and clouds puffed into animals or castles or people's faces. The wind blew our short hair, and the promise of coolness forced our arms outside the car to catch more relief from the sultry evening. Always Mother noticed and ordered, "Get your arms inside the car!"

On particular evenings after store hours, we sat at the rectangular table covered with embroidered muslin in the nook of the green and white kitchen. We ate our supper of red sockeye salmon, deviled eggs and cold *philabunk* (sour cream sprinkled with sugar and cinnamon). Papa and Mama were tired, Ruth and I restless with anticipation.

"When can we leave?" we asked. "Soon, please? Can we leave pretty soon? It's hot. Please hurry."

Our parents finished their coffee at what seemed a painfully leisured pace. When Mother began stacking the dishes in a large aluminum dishpan, we flew down the back stairs, carefully holding the back porch screen door so it wouldn't slam or let flies into the back porch where we kept the three-burner kerosene stove and the electric washing machine. The door secure, we raced to the Dodge.

With bathing suits and white caps with chin straps rolled tightly in our bath towels, we rode a mile west and turned the corner south. Out of town, only an occasional tree broke the reaching landscape—a tree, a fence row, or the little cluster of buildings that marked a far-off farm.

After an eternity of sweltering back seat, we arrived at Twin Lake for an evening swim. Finally, finally! Papa swam a strong and even breast stroke that never varied. He never removed his glasses. Mother used a slow side stroke. Ruth swam the dog paddle faster than anyone I ever knew. Together we practiced our strokes.

When our parents had had enough, Ruth and I were allowed to stay in longer, but we knew we would be called out of the water soon. We played—turning somersaults under water, diving through each other's legs, testing our ability to stay under water. Our mother's voice came to us from shore and we dove, knowing that she couldn't expect us to hear her under water, knowing that when we ran out of air the swim would be over. Our best breath holding al-

ways came on that last dive. Then we burst into the warm
air, gasping.

"Time to come in, girls! Edith. Ruth. All right, girls,
come."

Evening closed in. There was no avoiding the final call.
"It's getting dark. Come in. Come in."

Blessed coolness of the night air and driving home in
the soft summer dark. I twisted a bit of hair in front of each
ear, held it firmly and checked with Ruth to see if I had a
good spit curl.

*   *   *

Sometimes we drove to that same Twin Lake for a base-
ball game on Sunday afternoons. The Trimont team (players
came from both villages) played Welcome or Dunnell or
Sherburn. I stood on the side of the field, holding my body
and waving my arms in imitation of the catcher or the umpire.
I heard Uncle Oscar yelling, hurrahing or booing. Papa never
became much involved.

The women, in flowered cotton dresses, sat and talked
on the grass. Kids ate snacks and drank pop, begging for permission to go swimming. "Later. Later," said the mothers.
"You must wait until the ballgame is over and you can be
supervised in the water."

Into the woods we ran. A part of the shoreline had steep
banks, and we played follow-the-leader up and down, zig-zag-
ing back and forth, under tree branches that sometimes hit us
in the face, jumping over patches of poison ivy. My bare legs
were scratched by weeds and branches. My face grew hot,
sweat rolling down my cheeks and into my eyes. The leader
made the trail difficult; when someone fell, we laughed.

*   *   *

In the summertime, our mother took Ruth and me to
Minneapolis for several weeks to see Mormor (our mother's
mother), and our old neighbors, the Dickinsons, the high-
light of every summer. The house where we had once lived
became a second home.

The journey on the Minneapolis-St. Louis train was

sooty, hot and included a stopover in Winthrop. A miniature faucet with its companion container of long, white-paper cups located at the far end of the train car kept us busy walking back and forth for water. We read and colored. If I spied a white horse in a field we passed, I would make a wish, spit on the middle finger of my right hand, slap it into the palm of my left, clench my fist and pound the spot. Only then would my wish come true.

Mormor was fragile but vigorous, always in motion. The fragrant loaves of white bread that came from her oven did not have to cool before being sliced, and we (including Evelyn Dickinson) were allowed large hunks while the steam still rose from the bread, the heat melting gobs of butter. We laughed at each other, and the butter ran down our chins. If glasses of milk, poured from metal syrup pails in the ice box, tipped over, Mormor did not scold.

*   *   *

Mama went shopping with Nora Dickinson. Evelyn was at Mormor's with us for the day. Mormor, worn out from her frenetic activity, sat on her rocker on the open porch. Ruth, Evelyn and I anchored our bottoms on the sidewalk, legs spread wide apart, playing jacks. How pleased we were when we could control that tiny hard rubber ball. It had such a bounce. Babies, baskets, half cast, whole cast, and all ten jacks scooped up successfully. Mormor was not interested in our game. She rocked, Swedish psalm book resting in her lap. Evelyn, who was very good at jacks, taught Ruth and me new variations to introduce to our Triumph friends.

Another day we played dolls at Evelyn's house, only two blocks up the street. Evelyn had a new doll, Sigrid. Like her other big doll, Gertrude, Sigrid had real hair and was larger than any of the dolls Ruth or I had.

As we played, we gradually left the dolls and interested ourselves in books. We read about the Bobsey Twins and raided Bruce's bookcases too. He teased us, and we pretended to be mad but continued to provoke him to gain his attention.

We roller skated on the wooden front porch until Mrs.

Dick chased us off onto the cement sidewalk. Up and down and around the block, we danced on the noisy ball-bearing skates. When a skate came loose, we hunted madly for the square-nosed skate key. A race, a fall, and a skinned knee, the rough brown scab that formed grew thicker and thicker and lasted all summer.

Later, we moved on to lipstick and the Charleston. We took the streetcar to Lake Calhoun where Ruth and I showed off our Australian crawl stroke to Evelyn. Sunburned, hot and very tired, we finally caught the St. Louis Park streetcar home. We wished we could spend our streetcar fare for pop. One day we gave in to that fancy and walked all the way home. Never again.

On other trips downtown, we rode bright yellow streetcars with pale yellow cane seats that looked as though they had been braided and left funny marks on our legs. Above the windows, we read aloud fascinating advertisements for Prince Albert chewing tobacco, Lydia Pinkham's pills, and Karaghuesan rugs—in the ad a fat brown man sat cross-legged on his Persian carpet. Downtown, at Woolworth's Dime Store, we wandered through aisles of counters—bracelets of gold and silver, cosmetics in the tiniest packages, red and pink lipstick, Lady Grey rouge and eye shadow, teensy bottles of perfume, Cutex nail polish, as well as the jacks and marbles and miniature doll furniture that still attracted us.

After we returned to Triumph, the Minneapolis visit tales gave Ruth and me a certain distinction. We had new books and new little dolls and told our friends about going to the Orpheum Theatre, where, in addition to a movie, we saw seven or nine acts of real-live people performing—silly songs, jugglers, beautiful dancing girls in fantastic costumes, funny black-faced men who told jokes we tried desperately to remember.

*   *   *

On my twelfth birthday, Papa pulled the lens of his Kodak camera forward, opening the black, pleated cloth like an accordian. He took a picture of me standing in front of the

Edith, age twelve.

scrubby pine trees that bordered the shore of Potato Lake. Feet apart, one knee slightly bent, my right hand raised over my eye as though I were looking into the distance, I posed in what Papa felt was an unposed stance. The breeze that blew the tie of my long-sleeved white middy blouse could not move my hair, cropped in a real boy haircut. I wore dark knickers buttoned tightly below the knees, long ribbed stockings, and Mary Jane sandals. I was pleased with my going-camping outfit.

*   *   *

In bed on summer evenings, my sunburned ears hot and sore, I listened. June bugs whirred against the screen. Drowsy, half asleep, I recognized the delicious scent of cigar smoke drifting up from the street. Voices, laughter. I couldn't quite hear, but even when I almost made out the words, I did not understand the joke. I slid toward sleep, enjoying the softness of the night. Summertime.

Part II

5.

"She Never Did Get to California"

When I was little, Mama was always there. Mama *was.* The verb "to be." Enough to know. When she died, I said to Ruth, "Poor Mother, she never did get to California."

Ruth nodded her head. "I know. I know. Poor dear Mother. She never did get to California."

I knew an uneasy ache.

When I die, I do not want my daughters saying, "Poor dear Mother, poor dear Mother, she never did get to Greece."

So, in 1969 I borrowed money to go to Greece and made an overseas journey each year for the next fourteen years. When I die, my daughters will say, "Poor dear Mother. There's twenty-five dollars in the Twin City Federal Savings and Loan she didn't spend."

I'll save the United States for my old age. By 1984 I had been to London six times, Paris three times, Nairobi and the Outer Hebrides and Tokyo and Russia and other faraway places, and I had spent eight days in New York and saw Ellis Island and the Lady of Liberty. I thought about my mother and knew once more an uneasy ache.

* * *

The doctor and his wife, Joe and Gracie Butz, who lived in our small town, made a trip to California. My mother, who had grown up in Sweden, that northern land of long nights and cold, found their stories romantic: endless days of sunshine, palm trees and ocean. She used to talk to Papa, Ruth and me about a dream she had, a future time when we had made enough money in the store to drive to California and see that golden land.

Mother was a great reader. Mastering the English language, she wore out two dictionaries. Every day she read the Bible and the Christian Science textbook, *Science and Health with Key to the Scriptures* by Mary Baker Eddy. But her reading did not stop there. She read the newspapers, and she read novels. I see those novels lined up behind the glass doors of the wide mahogany bookcase—Glynn and Southworth and Fox. She read *The Woman's Home Companion* and *The Delineator,* worrying over the fate of the heroines whose stories were serialized in the monthly issues of those magazines. And she read the yellow-covered *National Geographic* magazines that eventually became high piles in our storeroom. Her curiosity was boundless. Many times I saw her look at the moon and heard her wonder, "Are there people on the moon? Would anyone ever know?" I thought of her when Neil Armstrong stepped on that soil in 1969!

Mother was sixty-four years old when she died. I never really heard her life's story. Not all of it.

"Let the dead bury the dead," she said. "The past is done and gone. We are living in America now, the New World."

How I wish she had written down her thoughts or even told me more stories about her growing up years in Sweden on that farm in Löderup whose edges were the shoreline of the Baltic Sea.

I left home at seventeen. Every week she wrote me a letter. I see her now, sitting at the dining room table—that table with its bulbous legs—writing to me, just as I had seen her write letters to her father and mother on Sunday evenings. Often she included paragraphs or sections of an article she had copied from *The Christian Science Sentinel* or *The Christian Science Monitor,* statements she thought would interest or inspire me in my life at school or as a young mother.

I don't have a single one of her letters! How could I have been so careless? Didn't I know that one day she would die and leave me? My recipe box in the kitchen has a few cards in her handwriting. Treasures.

* * *

I have seen the farm where my mother grew up. In Löderup, at the southern tip of Sweden, a lush green section known as the Riviera of Viking Land. Her father's name was Nels Olson. He married Kjersti Mortenson, and they had seven children. Two died. My mother, Bessie, was the third of the five living children: Martin, Ella, Bessie, Anna, and John.

Some fragments of my mother's growing up I have from her: laughing and singing while skating in winter on bright moonlit nights, swimming in the Baltic Sea in the summer. The happy Christmas time when the children received a story book and a small bag of candy at the church festivities; at home they found that St. Nicholas had left each of them an orange. Best of all were the story books. If her father did not get drunk on Christmas Eve, that was the best of all.

Bessie loved her years in the small country school in Löderup. Those years ended when she finished the eighth grade and, confirmed in the Lutheran Church, she went to work for a veterinarian as a hired girl. She hated it. Aunt Anna recalled that Bessie said she was so homesick that she thought she would die. One of the best days of her life was when she spilled boiling water on her foot and was forced to quit the job and go home.

My mother's other sister, my Aunt Ella, fell in love with a blacksmith apprentice, Oscar Westerdahl, who had an uncle in America. By 1903 this uncle had brought Oscar to Illinois. Oscar worked at the Moline Plough Company long enough to earn passage for his bride to be and Bessie. Life in Sweden had been difficult; life in America would be better; the sisters came. Of their journey from Löderup to Moline, I know nothing.

In the New Country, Bessie and Ella worked as hired girls. Bessie's beginning wage of $1.00 a week finally grew to $3.50. Two dollars went into an imitation leather coin purse. Bessie's savings. The purse had metal clasps that clicked when she opened it and clicked when it was shut. She kept it in a candy box with red roses on the cover. A reddish stain beside the roses marked where a red satin ribbon once had been tied. In time, her nest egg, with the help of Ella's savings, grew large enough to pay their father's passage from the Old Country to Moline. He found work in a Moline factory, learned enough English to get along, and was happy to be in a city filled with people to talk to, laugh with, and drink with.

Ella married Oscar. Bessie continued to work as a hired girl in Moline. Her imitation leather coin purse clicked and clicked. She was saving money for a visit home, though, from time to time, she sent money to her mother. Anna remembered that their mother once bought a sofa with $5.00 that Bessie sent her. Bessie kept adding money to the imitation leather purse in the candy box, and, one day in 1908, she had enough money for a round-trip ticket home to Sweden.

Although my mother never talked about it, Anna said Bessie had a wonderful summer. In 1980 my sister and I went to Sweden. There we talked with Ola, a young cousin of our mother's. Ola recalled Bessie's visit of that summer, a very important event in the village. As we stood under an ancient oak in the church yard in Löderup, Ola told us how he, a young lad then, had climbed that very tree to watch the dancing and games during Bessie's visit home. He said, "She was so beautiful in her pretty American clothes and had such a happy time."

Anna also added that during the summer, a certain young man, son of a blacksmith, paid my mother a great deal of attention. He even followed her to America with the intention of marrying her. "But," said Anna, "it was all wrong. Bessie had a hard time getting rid of him." I suspect my mother might have said that he had too much of the Old Country about him.

During that visit home, Bessie decided that "something must be done about brother Martin." Oldest of the children, Martin had served his time in the Swedish army. In pictures of him as a young man, I see him standing tall in his trim uniform with braid and brass buttons. His shining black eyes heavily fringed, his hair black and very sleek, his mustache curled at the edge, he was very handsome. The corners of his mouth turned up just enough to suggest he was about to smile. Martin inherited his father's outgoing nature and his father's love for alcohol and women. He had no sense of responsibility. What the immediate problem was that made it necessary that he leave Sweden, I do not know, but leave he must. And there was my mother with enough money in her purse to pay passage for him across the ocean. She even gave him her gold watch.

In a few weeks he returned to Löderup with this story: "I went to Ellis Island, but they refused to let me into America." Later, he was forced to admit that he had lied. The truth was that he had gone as far as Copenhagen, where he had had a "gay old time" spending all the money Bessie had given him, even selling her gold watch. A month later my mother *bought* his ticket and sent him off. This time he made it to America.

Uncle Martin was always my favorite uncle. I remember as a small child sitting on his lap while he read to me, and his wiping my tears when I cried over the plight of "The Little Match Girl." He gave me piggyback rides, bought me ice cream cones, had candy for me in his pocket. He had three wives, three or four legitimate children (I've lost these cousins), and various affairs. He borrowed money from his aging parents and never repaid them. During World War II, he went to California where he worked in a munitions plant. Finally, pensioned in California, he lived with a woman who ran a boarding house. When I was thirty-nine, he visited me, my husband, Paul, and our children. He told us about the woman with whom he lived, and how he helped her out by doing small chores about her house. He died in 1953 and was buried in California.

When Bessie returned to the States, her sister Anna sailed with her on the *Iverne*, a ship later sunk by the Germans. Anna told the story about a butcher from Brooklyn who fell in love with Bessie on the ship, and "she had a good time with him, too." But he was not the "right one" for Bessie either. "Didn't have your mother's *class*," Anna said.

Bessie lived in Moline until 1910 or 1911, when she moved to Minneapolis to be near the Westerdahls. After an unhappy two or three months as cook for the Atkinson family, Bessie went to work as a linen girl at the Hastings Hotel. There, Mrs. Gorrian, wife of the hotel owner, took an interest in her and asked her to come to work as an upstairs maid in her home. Now, when I drive downtown through Kenwood and Lake of the Isles, I stop at the intersection of Euclid Place and Irving Avenue and look at the house where my mother worked as a maid.

Last of the family in Sweden, Bessie's mother, Kjersti, and the youngest son, John, came to this country. Everyone contributed money for their passage. Anna, John, Bessie and Martin lived with their parents in a rented house in St. Louis Park. Kjersti kept house; everyone else worked. Finally, they were all together.

Bessie traveled to America, to Moline, to Minneapolis— even back home for a visit to Sweden—but no, my mother never did get to California.

6.

She Was Somebody

I think about my mother and my grandmother—their immigration. These women were not Moberg and Rolvaag heroines, homesteaders who trekked across the prairies to break ground, but they left familiar shores to sail on slow ships across a wide ocean to a strange land with customs and a language they did not understand.

I try to imagine what it was like for them. My mother was young and traveled with her sister. How about Grandma? Over fifty years old, alone with her young son? What was it like for her? Were others she knew on the ship? Was she scared? How could she not have been?

My mother called her Mor. We called her Mormor until we grew older and then called her Grandma. We took her for granted. I never knew her to have a friend outside the family. Who ever wondered if she was happy? Did she ever think about her own happiness or the lack of it? What went on inside her head? What tears wet her pillow?

Her family was not only the center but the circumference of her universe. It seems to me that she rested happily right there. I suspect that her preoccupation with the primary needs of her family kept her from being unhappy. She would never have been able to understand her female grandchildren and great grandchildren sitting around with a group of women discussing happiness and making positive statements such as, "*I must take the responsibility for my own happiness.*" Certainly she was virtuous in the Aristotelian sense in which virtue is defined as altruism, thinking mostly about the needs of other people.

I see Mormor sitting in a small rocking chair next to a hard-coal heater in the front room of the house on Brunswick Avenue in St. Louis Park. The red glow from the isinglass reflected in the thin skin of her wrinkled cheeks. Her hair, scraped back tightly from her face and protruding ears, discouraged wrinkles in her forehead. Made them impossible. Her rimless spectacles kept sliding down the narrow bridge of her small, sharp nose. Deep-set dark brown eyes under heavy brows looked at me over her glasses. She told me that never, never in all her life, had life been so good, so easy. She sighed, a kitten-purr of contentment, almost complacency.

She wore black—a dress with a high collar and long skirt. Peeking from under the skirt were high black shoes. In the kitchen she wore a long gingham apron tied about her waist, but sitting in the rocker—rocking, rocking, rocking— she held the tiniest of worn leather books in her hands, the Swedish Psalm Book. Books and newspapers always lay scattered about her house, but I never knew Mormor to read anything other than the thin, yellowed pages of the tiny Psalm book.

When my mother lay dying, she looked at her own hands on the white sheet of the hospital bed and said, "I used to think my hands were so ugly. Now, as I lie here dying, I think of all these hands have done."

Did Mormor, sitting in her rocker with the Psalm book in her hands, ever have such thoughts? *Her* hands had milked cows, plucked chickens, woven cloth, weeded sugar beet fields, tatted miles of lace, baked thousands of loaves of bread, wiped many noses and bottoms . . .

My grandmother, Kjersti Mortenson, was Somebody. Never mind that her father was a large landholder in Sweden,

Mormor and Forfor, my grandparents, Kjerste and Nels Olson.

a country where few owned land, she was a farmer's daughter and uneducated. The story is that my grandfather, Nels Olson, married the twenty-six-year-old Kjersti for her property—several large, fertile farms. Seven babies were born. Two died in infancy.

Nels was a handsome, good-natured, sociable dreamer, a man who found his greatest pleasures in reading and writing. He was a great storyteller. He was not a farmer. His lack of attention to the business of the land and his drinking parties with his many men friends finally resulted in the loss of all the farm property.

On my table every Christmas, I spread a cloth—hand woven in brilliant red and green and blue. The monogram "M" in one corner saved it from the household auction when the farm was lost. Articles that bore monograms of the owner were exempt from sale. My Aunt Anna remembered: "That was a sad day. They lost the farm, left it, and moved into the little old house, #12 in Löderup. Our mother went out and worked in the sugar beet fields for other people. Tied bundles. We all worked in the fields. Dig up the beets, cut them off, throw them in piles. Dig up . . . cut off . . . throw . . ."

Anna told another story of that time. Kjersti had a sister living on a neighboring farm. Very well off, this sister's husband was "a stingy, mean old man." At secret midnight rendezvous, in a neighboring field, the sister would bring Kjersti flour, salt, potatoes, and other food.

Two daughters immigrated to Moline, Illinois. When they sent money for their father's passage, Nels joined them in Moline. He found work in the machine shop of the John Deere Company, worked faithfully and was promoted to foreman. Left alone with her two youngest children, Kjersti continued in the beet fields, waiting for her husband to send money for her and the children to come to America. Anna left with Bessie. Finally, her son-in-law and children—not her husband—sent the money. She came. She came, and she conquered. Loneliness, poverty, and, not quite but almost, the language—she conquered.

My grandparents lived in a typical wooden prairie house, painted grey. It had a screened-in front porch where we sat on warm summer evenings and listened to whippoor-wills call. In the back yard was a vegetable garden; from the kitchen window Grandma could see sweet corn growing tall. No close neighbors. In the front room (where Mormor rocked with her Psalm book), a couch rested against the north wall. The loose cover on it was muddy-red and green-striped; portieres of this same cloth—as tough as burlap, as heavy as carpet, and scratchy to the touch—had been woven in Sweden and made a closet door upstairs.

A library table stood on the living room's east wall in front of a large window. Behind the coarse, ecru-colored lace curtains that hung on that window were dark green shades. When the sun shone brightly, pin pricks of white light peeked through. A small radio sat among Swedish and American newspapers and magazines (*Popular Mechanics*, *Saturday Evening Post* and a Swedish-English dictionary) on an ecru linen runner embroidered in purple, green and yellow silk. On one wall, a black and white picture of three magnificent white horses, necks raised high, running into the wind, their manes flying, gave life and movement to this quiet room. Lording over all, a large portrait of Grandpa—a bulbous man with a great shock of dark hair and eyebrows so thick as to serve as shades for his shining brown eyes—dominated the room.

An archway on the south side of the living room opened into a bedroom. My grandmother's portrait hung there—stern, unsmiling, high-cheek-boned face, head raised, supported by the stiff neck encased in a white ruff. Serious and wise and courageous. That is how she looked to me and how I think of her.

On the large brass bed with a white spread inset with hardinger lace that my grandmother had made on a wooden loom, Grandma napped afternoons. After twenty minutes or so, she would say, in Swedish, "Yah, if I am going to live, I better get up and live."

On the round table in the kitchen we ate the meals Grandma fixed on her wood-burning stove—bacon and eggs at any time of the day, pork roasts with apple sauce, pot roast with dark-brown carrots, stewed chicken, mutton and

lamb stews, and stacks of homemade bread. At my grandmother's table, if food remained, she would say, "Oh, you
didn't like it!" but if we cleaned every platter and bowl, she
said, "Oh, there wasn't enough!" For breakfast the morning
of my wedding day, I ate her Swedish meatballs at this table.

At this same table, my heavy, tall—I think it fair to call
him massive—grandfather lined sheets of white paper for
writing. Against the edge of a steel ruler, he ran his strong
thumbnail across the paper before writing letters to relatives
in Sweden, his daughters Anna, Ella, and Bessie. From his
seat at the table or the couch in the living room, Grandfather
uttered pontifical statements. Tiny eighty- to ninety-pound
Mormor scurried about like a small chicken, giving the im-
pression that she was doing as he asked, taking care of him.
We knew that even in big matters, she had learned to dis-
regard his authoritarian commands. When his farts became
especially pungent, she sprinkled sugar on the top of the
warm cook stove.

Not many people knew Grandmother. But, being Somebody did not mean that many people needed to know her.
I don't think she struggled with self-doubt. She was courageous
and strong; she had spirit and guts, and, if she had been asked,
I think she would have agreed that she was proud of herself.
Oh, she could tell her husband off when he became too much
for her. "Forbaskad man!" she would say and go her way,
disregarding male members of the family. At the age of
eighty-seven, she still ran up and down the stairs to the
damp cellar for crocks of butter or pickled beets.

St. Louis Park was sparsely settled, "out in the boon
docks," some said. Grandfather walked to Hamilton's General
Store several times a week for salt or sugar or Jell-O and his
Luden's cough drops. He walked to the Post Office every
morning. Once a week, Grandmother took off for Witt's Meat
Market in downtown Minneapolis. I can picture her walking
briskly in her sturdy, high shoes, her long black skirt swinging,
to the streetcar line. She carried a big brown shopping bag.
After walking ten blocks to the carline, she paid her five-cent
fare for the hour ride to Seventh and Hennepin, where,
standing on the sawdust-covered floor in front of glass
counters, she considered carefully her purchases of pot roast,

Swedish sausage, bacon and chicken. From her half-moon, cracked, leather coin purse with metal snaps, she pulled out wadded bills to pay the butcher. He put the money in a little wire basket that went sailing overhead to the cashier on the mezzanine. Mormor then carried the heavy shopping bag to the streetcar stop and waited—the car ran only every thirty minutes. After riding to the end of the line, she carried her purchases the ten blocks home. As she unpacked the shopping bag, she sang Swedish hymns in a cracked voice.

When she was eighty-seven years old, she broke her hip and fell. ("Her hip broke, and so she fell," the doctor comforted us.) She had always been thin, and when I went to see her lying in the bed in the room off the living room, I thought I had never seen any person so fragile, so tiny, so wraith-like. She was in bed only a week. She died as she had lived—quietly, bravely, certain in her Lutheran faith that she would meet her God.

Oh, my Grandmother Mormor . . . she was Somebody.

*The Swedes in time proved themselves
exceptional among European peoples
in not harping on their former greatness.
They successfully and peaceably made
the transition from the role of a great
power to that of a small one.*

A History of the Modern World
Palmer and Colton

7.

I Remember Papa

Alfred Svente Johnson, Papa, was born in 1879 in Malmö, Sweden. His heritage and education rang with tales of Sweden's greatness: how the Swedes had produced a line of extraordinary rulers from Gustavus Adolphus to the contemporary King Oscar, how the Swedes had cut through the Holy Roman Empire and helped ward off the unification of Germany by the Hapsburgs, how a Swedish king claimed to be the king of Poland, and how Swedes won control of virtually all the shores and cities of the Baltic. When Papa was born, Norway was still a part of Sweden.

For Papa, the way things were done in the Old Country was always superior to the way they were done in America. Swedish customs must be observed; Swedish cooking was always preferred. When, before his marriage, American doctors prescribed surgery for a knee problem, Papa sailed to Sweden for the operation. He dreamed of earning a fortune in America, but returning to Sweden to spend it—a brick house, perhaps at Limhamn, a resort town near Malmö on the Baltic Sea.

An only child, Alfred's parents are faceless to me. His father was some kind of a wholesaler who owned large warehouses, some on the waterfront. I don't even know his parents' names. His father died when quite young, leaving his widow to raise little Alfred. When Papa was sixteen, his mother died of cancer. I think he grieved for her all his life. Even in his seventies, he would note the anniversary of his mother's birth and death.

I have but one picture of Papa as a child. His is one of many faces on a faded, sepia photograph of a confirmation class. Sixty-four black-costumed students, male and female, their backs ramrod straight, stare at me. The light-colored aprons worn by seven of the girl-women provide the only relief in the blackness. Thirteen figures in the front row hold their hands primly in their laps; stiff arms of the others hug their sides. So grave the expressions on all their faces, they might well be contemplating Lutheran hellfire and damnation. Sixty-four faces. I don't know which is Papa's.

Left without anything, I draw from my imagination for a picture of Papa as a child. I see a lonely little Alfred, slight and probably frail, fussed over and spoiled by his mother, still needing to be independent and confident. Perhaps his mother's unconditional love for him gave him his fine sense of self. Even at the lowest moments in his life, he never seemed to doubt his own superiority. He had no need to proclaim it to the world; his quiet assurance defined it.

I see the small boy hanging onto his mother's skirts. Large, round, blue eyes in a thin face—bookish, quiet—his mama's good little boy. Above average intelligence and nearsighted. It was hard to play ball with rowdy playmates when he could not see the ball. He probably spent much time with books, practicing his penmanship and nosing about the docks and harbor. He used to tell us the story of how he wandered about those docks, watching the big ships and the sailors. One day he found a pair of spectacles, put them on, and was amazed to see a whole new world open up before him. He saw trees in the distance along the shoreline, rooftops far over the city, and ships far out at sea—things before that had melded into softness without detail. "Wearing glasses," he told us, "was a shameful thing to do when I was a boy." He hid the glasses in a special place at the wharves; every afternoon after school, he went there alone, put on the glasses and looked and looked.

When his mother died, young Alfred came by ship to the United States. On the rare occasions when he talked about his arrival in Superior, Wisconsin, he told of an uncle who fed him weiners and mashed potatoes.

From the bookish little boy who loved school and reading, I see Papa grow into a slim young man working as a bookkeeper for a lumber company in Superior. With love I use and polish a metal napkin ring engraved "Superior, Wisconsin" within a circle of flowers and leaves, a souvenir from that time. While working for the lumber company, Papa traveled to Montana to be the accountant-paymaster for lumberjacks.

Papa liked to talk about his experiences as camp cook. When the cook of the lumber camp became ill, Papa took over his job. He made the finest buckwheat pancakes anyone had ever eaten, he told us, and his baking powder biscuits were not only hearty but light as a feather. Based on these stories, my mother once suggested he make buckwheat cakes for the family. He set the batter to raise one evening. The next morning, the yeasty mixture had overflowed the yellow, earthenware crock with the blue border, eked its way right out the porch window and paved a fine road down the sloping roof of the back porch of the store. Another time, when Mother was sick—really sick with the flu, sick enough to stay in bed!—Papa made vegetable soup. It simmered all day, and mother, smelling it, was grateful for his help as well as for the coming meal. When he brought her a bowl, she raised her bushy eyebrows, smiled a strange smile and coughed in a mild way. We ate our portions in silence. None of us could tell Papa that his soup was too salty.

After working for the lumberjacks, young Alfred eventually arrived in Minneapolis, where he worked as an accountant for a construction company and then the Yellow Cab Company. When he married Bessie Nelson, he kept books for the Brin Glass Company.

Not a small man, maybe, but certainly not big—mild-mannered and gentle—that's how I remember Papa. My earliest memories include his spanking me—but I have no memory of fear or pain, only gentleness and smoothness, like the new bark of the green sapling. The merest suggestion of a spanking. The need for him as parent to let me know I had done wrong. A more vivid memory is the touch of his soft hand, patting my arm as I lay sick in bed with a cold.

His hands were small. He liked wearing his opal ring on his right little finger and never removed the gold wedding band or the Masonic ring from his slender fingers. The only callous on his perfect hands was the bump from holding a pen. After polishing the brass candlesticks he had brought from Copenhagen, he said, "Feel . . . feel how smooth this brass." He liked to touch the silk shirt mother made him. On buying trips to the Cities, he indulged in Turkish baths at the West Hotel.

There was nothing of the macho man about Papa. He was strictly a sidewalks and big buildings person who never extoled the glories of nature, the wonder of the wide open plains of Martin County, or desired life on a farm. Unlike many of his friends in Triumph, he never owned a gun or hunted or played tennis on Dr. Butz's tennis courts. A little quiet fishing, perhaps, time spent rowing his boat and the slow breast stroke at Twin Lake—these were pleasant activities for him.

He seldom raised his voice, and I never heard him yell at anyone, but, when angry, Papa's face grew red. He suffered from stomach ulcers and migraine headaches. He was never a really well man—dyspeptic might have been the word—but he wasn't gloomy. Critical, yes, but not cross. He was much concerned with his stomach and his bowels. When we returned to Triumph from our trips to Minneapolis, Papa's drugstore purchases always included Pluto Water—clear white bottles containing lightly tinted green liquid and sporting little red devils on the outside. When Papa lay on the bed with the shades pulled down, Ruth and I had to be very quiet.

With his keen sense of smell, he was always the first to detect any unpleasant odor. Nothing rotten stayed in the store. He bought Djier Kiss perfume for Mother and was not above using it on himself when the two of them went to a dance or card party.

He wore good shoes and kept them highly polished. He bought suits with vests, tailored in Minneapolis. Mother starched and ironed his shirts. A gold pocket watch stretched between his vest pockets on a heavy, gold chain. When his hair began to grey, he secretly dyed it, and I can still picture him in front of the mirror combing the thining black locks.

"Mama" turned into "Mother" for Ruth and me, but "Papa" remained forever "Papa." This Papa, however, had as much dignity as any "Father." Alistair Cook on Masterpiece Theater always reminds me of him. Papa had a face like Cook's.

Papa read *National Geographic* magazine and Swedish newspapers and collected leather- and vellum-covered Swedish books and the coins in the glass-doored bookcase. He liked dogs, especially German police dogs. We had, in succession, four of them. Reno had to be put to sleep at a relatively early age due to incurable mange. I can still smell the sulphur we lived with for months before that sad day. Reno II failed to look carefully when crossing the street one day. Reno III refused to stop killing sheep on Farmer Bernhardt's farm just south of town; he had to be destroyed.

Papa knew how to cry and did so occasionally, but unabashedly at the death of his dogs. I remember the four of us sitting at our breakfast table, tears running down all four faces. Reno IV grew old gracefully. He became attached to one of Ruthie's boyfriends and, shortly after Ruth left home, spent more time there than at the store. We were spared the grief of Reno IV's expiration.

I can picture Papa in his brown overstuffed arm chair in the living room in Triumph, light coming from the west window at noon. Next to him stood a cigarette stand with a heavy glass tray and a green and white package of Lucky Strike cigarettes. The package never left the stand; Papa never smoked in the store. After listening to the market reports on the Freid Eisman radio and eating his lunch, he would have a short, quiet time in that chair smoking a cigarette. Even that he did elegantly. No cigarette dangling from his lips! When he smoked, the act itself held his full attention.

Or I see him sitting in that same chair on Saturday night after the store finally closed. The light came then from the bridge lamp with the rose-colored silk shade Mother had sewn. A bottle of beer sat on the floor beside him. He occasionally tipped the bottle to his lips. Smoking a cigarette, he talked with Mother, who sat on the tapestry-covered footstool, swinging one foot. They discussed the business, the customers, profits, and bills.

My parents talked with each other a lot. Bessie was close to the operation of the store. Following supper, after Ruth and I were excused from the table, Papa and Mama sat for a long time drinking their coffee and talking. They talked about Mother's parents in St. Louis Park (Papa sent them money often), affairs of the town, what the competition down the street was doing, what might be put on sale the next week, and what Ruth and I might be allowed to do or not do. For the most part, they seemed to agree on discipline for us. As marriages go, theirs was probably better than average. Bessie was Papa's best friend.

Though I know they cared deeply for each other, and I have no doubt of the fidelity of their marriage vows, embraces and kisses between them were few and far between. That was not the Scandinavian way. What was, was how Papa belittled Mother in a kind of good-natured way we laughed about—the northern European male way, seeing himself as lord and master of the house, all knowing, domineering. Laughter made it easier to bear but did not diminish the hurt. Maybe this was why, when mother lay dying and wondering about the afterlife, she said to me, "I don't know what's ahead . . . but I don't think I want to be married to Alfred in the next life." Maybe, adventurous woman that she was, she only expressed a taste for something new. In this world, she excused Papa by saying, "Oh, that's just his way . . ."

Though she lay dying, and maybe considered spending eternity in some other way than how she had lived, mother repeatedly urged me, "Be sure that when you fix chicken and dumplings for Papa, put it on one large platter. Put the dumplings around the outside. He loves dumplings, and that's the way he likes them served." And, "Be sure that Papa always keeps the pale green and white blanket that came from Sweden, because it is heavy and warm, and he often gets cold at night."

8.

My Parents' Life in Triumph

When the Triumph Embroidery Club had its annual picnic at Fox Lake Park for the families of its members, Papa always selected carefully from the munificence of the board. Only the chicken our mother had fried or the potato salad she had made, or the prune cake that he knew came in the square pan belonging to us. When the event was over and our little family of four sat around the breakfast table having cocoa before bed, Papa would make fun of how "poor and white" other women's chicken looked, not "brown and beautiful" like Mother's.

Card playing formed a common recreation. Papa and Mama taught Ruth and me to play whist, then 500, and then auction bridge. We even graduated to contract bridge. I have no memory of competition—that is, any two of us against the other pair—but this kind of winter-evening fun carried into our married lives: Papa and Mother playing bridge with Tryg and Ruth and with Paul and me.

Papa loved to play cards. He played with "cronies" (mother's word) in Triumph. Sometimes he would bring mother the magnificent sum of twenty dollars that he had won in poker at the pool hall. Card parties were social events, sometimes involving four or eight people. I remember Sunday dinners when several couples had been invited. The men had a little *brännvin* before dinner, and the women laughed and scurried about the kitchen, mashing potatoes and making gravy to go with the turkey or fried chicken or pot roast. After coffee and cigars at the table, the women cleaned up while the men continued to puff their fine cigars. The laughter, cigar smells, and the sound of cards slapping the table continued long after Ruth and I were put to bed.

Drinking meant festivities and celebrations, fun and companionship. Papa liked to drink. As a child I thought life would be perfect if only I did not have to take music lessons and if only Papa never took a drink. Clearly, his drinking made me uncomfortable.

A bottle or two of brown whiskey always stood in the kitchen cupboard, and, during Prohibition, a truck delivered shiny metal gallon containers of alcohol late at night. Some Papa kept; some he sold to his friends. Whenever Papa drank whiskey, elegant, graceful Papa became foolish. He told jokes that Ruth and I did not find funny. Mother hated it.

One grey November Sunday with a mean wind howling and rattling the window panes and flakes of snow whirling by, Papa went down to the store early in the morning to work on his books. Behind the isinglass of the nickle-plated heater in the dining room, red coals glowed. Apple pies, warm from the black kitchen stove's oven, cooled on the kitchen cabinet. The aroma of roasting chicken filled the house. Ruth and I had left our school work and books to peel potatoes and set the dining room table. When the potatoes were done and mother was about to make the gravy, she ordered, "Call Papa."

I turned the black handle on the wall phone around once, paused, turned it again—the code for the store that did not involve the town's one telephone operator. No answer.

Mother took a turn at the phone. She executed one forceful ring and asked Central to call Dettmer's Pool Hall. Papa probably played poker with the boys.

"Is Alfred Johnson there?" she asked. The reply was negative, but mother continued talking. "If he comes around, tell him dinner at home is ready."

Papa appeared soon, and we all knew he had been drinking. Mother's utter disgust was also evident, and I remember being torn between sharing her displeasure and feeling sympathy for Papa.

But I must have felt more than embarrassment at his silliness, or the memories and feeling I have do not ring true. One of Papa's friends, Paul Hawkin, a Swedish drinking companion, was best man at my parents' marriage. (A porcelain cocoa set—a high, narrow pot and eight tall, fluted cups decorated with tiny pink roses, all carefully wrapped in tissue—now resting on my closet shelf was Hawkin's wedding present.) I have an early memory of standing at the front door of our little house in St. Louis Park with Mama. I was beside her and very close to the floor. The door opened, a cold draft pushing in. Papa, wearing a long, black overcoat, entered. He had just come home in a taxicab. In a low voice and with sadness as well as disgust, Mama said, "Oh, that Hawkins. Oh, that drinking."

*　　*　　*

Not a gregarious man, Papa was a private person—not an introvert, but not social. Perhaps he was shy. One evening at supper, Papa complained to mother that he had not been invited to participate in some special event of the Triumph Commercial Club. Mother said, "But, Alfred, you know that you would not have enjoyed that."

"No," Papa said, "but I would like to have been invited."

The phrase became a longtime family joke.

Papa was, however, zealously loyal to his friends. One of those, Ernest Krook, whom he may have known in Sweden, was a cabinet builder with an interest in and talent for photography. We have family portraits done by him. Krook could never save enough money to bring his wife and two young boys, Axel and Otto, to this country. Papa finally sent the passage money to his wife, Meja, and the children. The 1847 Rogers silverware we used for our Sunday dinners was an expression of their gratitude. Meja found work as a furrier, and they bought a house in south Minneapolis. The friendship between our two families survived the move to Triumph.

Whenever we came to Minneapolis, we visited the Krooks. I recall the trip on the streetcar—a Sunday expedition. Upon our arrival, amidst laughter and rapid-fire talk, the adults lapsed into Swedish. The men drank *brännvin*, and Papa told Krook stories of the store. After Meja's lavish dinner (mashed potatoes flavored with nutmeg, to my disappointment), the Krook boys, older than Ruth and I, were excused to go about their own activities. The adults played cards. Ruth and I fell asleep to the sounds of card playing, laughter and cigar smoke. Later, we woke for the long trip home to Grandmothers. In the dark night, as we stood on Lake Street waiting for a streetcar, a dark-faced Oriental dressed in jewel colors and seated cross-legged on a cushion glared at us from a lighted billboard. He advertised Persian rugs. I was scared.

Uncle Oscar Westerdahl was Papa's closest male friend. In our small community, the social life of my parents included Aunt Ella and Uncle Oscar. In addition to the large dinners and card parties, the two families shared picnics and all holidays. I close my eyes and, with little effort, see the four of them laughing. Oscar was a great storyteller.

Sometimes Papa and Oscar argued. The room quieted. Ella and Bessie suffered silently. Such tension was short-lived, however. The two men often conferred on business matters, loaned each other money, assumed the responsibility of their wives' parents in St. Louis Park and gossiped good naturedly about the natives of the towns and about the farmers in the surrounding countryside.

Another friend, Pete Frahm, owned the Frahm's Furniture Store directly across Main Street from our enterprise. Pete, also the town undertaker, lacked a funeral director's mien. I used to hear him come through the front door of the store in the morning.

"GOOD MORNING, ALFRED!" he would shout loud enough to wake the Bernhardt's on their farm south of town. Hearty, always jovial and good natured, Pete carried a paunch in front of him that made him tip slightly backwards as he walked. He always seemed to be taking on the whole world.

Despite their personality differences, he and Papa saw each other daily and enjoyed a close companionship. Papa talked with Mother about Pete's shortcomings (he had a hard time paying his bills) but always in a kindly and indulgent way.

Every Monday night, Papa and Pete went to Masonic Lodge meetings in the Community Hall, the same hall that housed visiting Chataquas—painted ladies, a fat man, golden-haired heroines and mustached villains, trunks and boxes of magic, and a whole band with shiny brass instruments. On those occasions, on the stage behind the blue and tan mountain scene on a canvas curtain that bumped and groaned going up and down, great drama unfolded.

The ladies of the Eastern Star, the female auxiliary of the Masonic Order, used this hall for a Mothers-Daughters Banquet. Although Mama did not have an enthusiasm for the Lodge equal to Papa's, she was one of the Star Points and Worthy Matron. At all these hall events, Masonic flags and emblems abounded. A podium with Masonic symbol on the front stood in full view in a corner, gavel in place.

To me, everything Masonic remained very secret. I wondered if Papa pounded on the podium with that gavel. Papa worked at getting people interested in the Lodge and once spent every evening for weeks, maybe months, helping Morrie Miller, husband of one of Mother's best friends, memorize the many words necessary to become a member.

Papa's tight hold on tradition and his past never was more evident than at Christmas, when we all had to rise at four o'clock in the morning to attend the *julotta* service at the Swedish Mission Church. Never mind that we never went to that Evangelical Lutheran Church at any other time of the year. Tired as we might be from our Christmas Eve festivities, we struggled from under our warm covers, dressed in our long underwear, warm sweaters, skirts and buckled overshoes to trudge sleepily through the dark morning. The snow crunched with every step. The memory of the candle-light and the singing and the words are hazy, but the spirit of the event remains clear. It was a Holy Time. God sent the Baby Jesus and All was Well.

I can imagine my mother moving along with new tra-ditions and eating oyster stew or even a standing rib roast on Christmas Eve. But not Papa! For him, Christmas Eve would not be Christmas Eve without Swedish meatballs, blood sausage, pickled beets, *sylta,* lutefisk, and *risgrynsgröt.*

Though times were both good and bad during the thirty years in the store, no one ever doubted that the move from Minneapolis to Triumph was wise. Our mother insisted that the years in Triumph, especially while Ruth and I were growing up, were very happy years for her. The store, our store, however, never recovered from the Depression. By the late 1930s and early 1940s, business had declined sharply. Papa's merchandizing methods, or lack of a method, could not compete with the modern chain store that moved into town. Automobiles carried farmers and townspeople to the larger towns of Fairmont and St. James for their shopping.

Ruth and I left to go away to school, to work and to marry. Mother wrote to us each Sunday night, came to visit us occasionally, rejoiced in our visits home, helped out in the store, and never complained.

Those years must have been grim for both of them, but my parents kept their financial worries to themselves. Papa slowly lost his air of optimism and made less use of one of his favorite words, "recoup." Having had some real victories in the stock market, it was hard for him to lose faith in his ability to recoup. They were a pair—Papa with his belief in himself and Mother's Christian Science optimism. Expenses, however, exceeded income during the last years. How frustrated they must have been! And lonely.

Years later, Mother told Ruth and me about one Christmas Eve in Triumph—one of the few years that neither of us came home. By the time she told us, Mother was able to smile about the evening.

"You know how Papa has always been about Christmas Eve," she said. "Even going to a movie on Christmas Eve was wrong. Christmas Eve was a sacred time. But this one year when we were alone, after we had eaten our lutefisk and opened our presents, Papa went 'down the street' and played cards. Can you imagine Papa doing that on Christmas Eve?" Smiling indulgently, she went on, "He probably just had that terribly lost feeling. . . ."

"Weren't you angry?" I asked. "Didn't you feel terrible?"

"No," she said. "I cleaned the kitchen stove."

*   *   *

One fine day in 1948, Papa sold the store for $10,000 cash. The move to Minneapolis was coming home. Mother was sixty-one, Papa, sixty-nine. I was thirty-four. My parents bought a charming white frame house at 4415 Thomas Avenue South; Lake Harriet was less than half a block away. Three good years followed. Mother said, "I didn't know that I would ever be so happy." Papa seemed relaxed and carefree. I saw them often. They enjoyed our children.

Then Mother died. Breast cancer. Papa lost his wife, his companion, his best friend of thirty-eight years. He was devastated.

He sat in the rocker in the living room of that lovely house so near the lake. "I think," he said, "of how she pumped water every Sunday night—soft water—for the Monday morning washing. Why didn't I help her?" He paused, then added, "But she could have asked me to help her."

The grief I suffered following Mother's death was a pain greater than I could ever have imagined. I am moved to remember with what fortitude Papa carried on with his life. He sold that house on Thomas Avenue and rented an apartment in a big old house near Lake and Hennepin. He set forth each day, taking a bus downtown or driving his little green Pontiac to our house. He kept himself immaculately clean, read the papers, and listened to the radio. Courageous and cheerful, sheer bravado at times. But lonely.

As to religion, Papa might have said that he carried a policy in Bessie's name. Confirmation in the Lutheran Church seemed to have left no dark or gloomy mark on him. I suspect that when he had finished with school at sixteen, he concerned himself with the literal and concrete business of numbers and accounting and gave little thought to heaven or God. Graciously tolerant of Mother's interest in Christian Science, he attended church with her while Ruth and I were in Sunday School. Mother used to say about Papa's going to church, "You can't pour water through a strainer without getting the strainer wet."

Mother also said that she didn't worry about Papa and religion, that his work in the Masonic Lodge kept him a good man and meant more to him than any other religious experience. Just once, after mother died, rocking in his dark, red-plush rocker, he questioned, "But, Edith, what if . . . what if this life is all there is?"

No certificate of death cites "broken heart" as the cause of expiration, but that is how I viewed Papa's death a year later. Ruth and I didn't even know he was dying. We knew only that he had been in surgery and that the operation on his ulcerated stomach had been a success.

I remember that Ruth and I sat together in the waiting room of the hospital. Sterile. Unreal. We talked and laughed, knowing a crazy euphoria because we had been allowed to sit there alone together—two young mothers with five young children. Hospitals. The smell, the click-click of the nurses' heels. Why didn't they all wear rubber heels? Or was there comfort in the sound of their footsteps? Comfort because someone was coming. Hildegarde Nelson from Triumph was a nurse then in the Minneapolis hospital. Ruth and I were glad mother was not with us. She was spared this.

We buried Papa beside mother in the grave he had bought while mother was dying. He had described the grave in Lakewood Cemetery to mother before she died: "We are on a small hill, beside the lake. Our heads will be higher than our feet, and we are very near the Westerdahls."

On Memorial Day, I polish the gravestones, arrange bouquets of iris or lilacs and stand looking at the lake. I remember . . . and I am filled with love and gratitude. There is an Essence . . . beyond Space and Time . . . Love.

Part III

9.

The Five Rs

I was seven years old when we moved to Triumph, sixteen when I graduated from high school. For ten years, for nine months of every year, life centered on what went on in and came from the Tri-Mont School. My education began: I learned about reading, 'riting, 'rithmatic, recreation, and relationships—the five Rs.

When I was a young mother and my daughters came home from the Edina School with their fine line of As on their report cards, I remember being told, "Some kids get a dollar for such good grades." I laughed and told them that their father and I expected such report cards of them. "After all, weren't both Dad and I valedictorians of our high school classes?"

When, years later, they found out that my high school graduating class only numbered thirteen people, they said I had been unfair. Who would consider thirteen people any kind of competition?

Since my daughters have grown, they have suggested that education in the Edina school system defined them as underprivileged, exposed only to the "higher socio-economic level," a limited experience. I cannot judge.

Thirteen in my graduating class; I grew up a Big Frog in a very small puddle. Seven hundred people lived in the twin villages of Triumph and Monterey that supported the four-room, red-brick schoolhouse. The Tri-Mont School stood sedately in the center of a large square block facing Main Street—in Triumph, to be sure, but bordered on the west by the street that bisected the two villages. Elm trees shaded the green lawn surrounding the school, except for the playground area and the softball diamond. From the towering metal flag pole, Old Glory waved.

How I loved school! Summers were fun, but no greater joy existed for me than beginning school each fall. Crossing the street from our store, I skipped three blocks west past King Oscar's small house, Meehan's house and Mayor Schwalen's big white house with the wide veranda. I was eager. Junior Mathewson, walking with Ruth and me, once said, "Why do you always look like your head is so far in front of the rest of your body?" Eagerness started there, didn't it? In the head? But after that, I often remembered Junior's words and tried hard to keep my back straight and walk slower.

Tri-Mont school. Four rooms. Two grades to a room. Grades one through four on the first floor; grade five defined a kind of coming of age in the school when those students, for the first time, had class upstairs. Sometimes my friend Evelyn Satter, a grade ahead of me, would be in my room, sometimes not. We rejoiced when we were together.

Seventh grade not only saw Evelyn and I in the same room, but brought us Mercedes Gugisberg for our teacher. A golden goddess. Statuesque, a coronet of golden braids, flashing blue eyes framed by long, light-brown lashes. Of Swiss descent and Catholic. Most everyone I had known had been German or Scandinavian and Lutheran. Fresh from Mankato Teachers College, she had energy and new ideas— basketball in gym class, popular songs in chorus, and Campfire Girls.

This last introduction presented a serious problem for Evelyn and me. She attended a German Lutheran church whose minister said the laws of her church absolutely forbade Evelyn from belonging to such an organization. We were devastated. Together in the same room again at last, her church was going to keep us from sharing this exciting new experience! But we were both well schooled in the "where there's a will, there's a way" philosophy of life. Long before we had learned that going to our parents with "Evelyn's mother said she could" and "Edith's mother said it was fine with her" helped immeasurably in allowing us to "stay over," go to the movies or take our bikes to the lake. Our calculated pleading found the way. Evelyn's parents called on the minister and announced that if Evelyn was not allowed to join Campfire Girls, she would be removed from the confirmation class and her parents would withdraw their support from the church. That settled the matter.

Miss Gugisberg taught her Wo-He-Lo girls all about work, health, and love. She convinced us of the importance of physical exercise, proper nutrition, and "true sportsmanship." We memorized the Campfire Girls laws—Seek Beauty, Be of Service, Be Healthy. I wrote a story about the beautiful rainbows in oil splashed on muddy streets and earned a Campfire bead.

The week after school let out, Miss Gugisberg took her eight Campfire Girls camping at Fox Lake Park near Sherburn. Hiking through the woods, we had lessons in the identification of leaves, trees, grasses and birds. We had crafts and swimming and campfires at night. At lunch we had whispered discussions about sex. Far from a perfect trip—it rained a lot and the days were perhaps too structured, demanding that we eat the beef stew we had written into the square that matched that day even with ninety-five degree temperatures—Fox Lake Park was memorable for the poem I wrote that pleased Miss Gugisberg: "The rain fell like silver needles."

Seventh grade was the year that I fell madly in love with Bud Johnson. With one crooked front tooth and the world's most engaging smile, he was the hero of my romantic dreams and the person I thought of as we sang Irving Berlin's "Always, always, I'll be loving you always . . ." and "Ain't he neat, comin' down the street . . ." But cruel fate, Bud was in love with Evelyn Satter. And they were both in the eighth grade. By the following year, an addition had been built onto the school so that we had a full-blown Trimont High School.

Evelyn and Bud were not only out of my room, but they were in high school. I was left behind.

But I still had to have one "best friend." In eighth grade that special person was Janet Storm. She had a pock-marked face and was too plump, but she was not dumb. We wrote long notes to each other, fantasized romantically of the future when Bud would love me and someone—a Magnificent Stranger—would fall in love with Janet. The world and life seemed all ahead, and we would make the most of it. I might write a book; I would never teach (except maybe swimming); or I might go live in the woods "next to Nature," but then I wanted to live in a big city. Janet sometimes called me silly, and I sometimes became impatient with her, but a mutual respect kept us good friends.

In eighth grade, however, Miss Gugisberg was replaced by small, dark-haired Florence Baker. Because she was not Mercedes Gugisberg, we were cruel to her, questioning her authority, even her information and knowledge. She must have overcome all that or we must have forgiven her for not being her predecessor, because I felt differently about her at the end of the term—even wrote letters to her later.

*   *   *

Calm years, these grammar school years seem in retrospect. The love of reading and writing became firmly instilled. Although neither mother nor Papa had had any formal education in English, their reward to themselves at the end of the day was reading. Winter evenings and Sunday afternoons often found Ruth on the floor with *The Eskimo Twins*, me with *Swiss Family Robinson*. Papa, in his big armchair by the window, read magazines or newspapers, and mother paged through her *Science and Health with Key to the Scriptures*, *The Christian Science Journal* or *The Delineator*.

Sometimes in the twilight of a cold winter evening, I know a nostalgia for that time: walking home from school after the blood-race of basketball practice or the excitement of Campfire meetings or with an armful of valentines. . . . I would race through the utter silence of winter snow to the yellow lights from our house, run upstairs to my mother and home.

10.

Freshman at Trimont High

The wind across the ripe wheat and barley fields south of Triumph blew soft and warm, but acorns lay scattered on the sidewalk. I was thirteen years old. A long awaited day had arrived; I was a freshman in high school.

Walking to school, skipping the cracks in the sidewalk as I always had, the new shoes felt tight; they almost hurt. New brown-and-white saddle shoes always made ugly red spots, sometimes blisters, on the back of my heels. But the sporty look of them with the white-ribbed ankle socks turned over just so blurred the pain. Besides, the rubber soles made me feel bouncy. And they complemented the brown and white plaid dress my mother had made for me for the first day of school. The dress had a white collar, a tight belt, and a pleated ruffle at the hem that swished when I walked.

I carried a notebook with a shiny three-ring binder, packs of glossy, neat paper, and a new Parker fountain pen filled with blue-black Scripto ink. The paper soon would be covered with notes from English I class—Shakespeare—and algebra problems (the mystery of letters mixed with numbers would soon be revealed) and Latin. Grades now broke into courses. We went to various rooms for classes, and the entire student body had desks in one large assembly room. Freshmen occupied two rows closest to the doors, furthest from the high windows opened with long poles. Brown wooden desks, solidly attached to the floor, with inkwells in the upper right corner.

But as exciting as all this wonderful grown-up newness was, the greatest part for me was the prospect of new teachers and new kids. Indeed, people bubble up, come to the top of my rose-colored memories of those years. Two especially: Velma Bolte and Miss Russ. Velma sat in the desk in front of me.

She was one of the country kids who came to Trimont High from a one-room country schoolhouse. Of German stock, Velma had a broad forehead, large, sensual lips, fair skin, light-brown hair and hazel eyes. She was without affectation, authentic. These were the characteristics in Velma that drew me and still draw me now.

With the other freshmen, I filed into algebra class. Velma and I sat next to each other in the second row and on the side of the room with high windows cut into the tan concrete walls. Our teacher was Ud Idstrom. He came from Gustavus Adolphus College in St. Peter, had gold in his front teeth, wore brown tweed suits and conservative ties. He made numbers and letters come alive. Sitting beside those windows in straight chairs with right armrests, Velma and I worked our problems together, came up with the right answers and discovered that we were both smart. And we were fascinated by our teacher. "When you marry," Velma wrote in a note secretly passed between us, "may you find a man with just that amount of yellow gold in his front teeth!"

In Miss Munson's Domestic Science class, we shared a work table. We learned the names and uses of the utensils, mastering also their arrangement in drawers. One day we began to cook. Together we carefully prepared a sugar-and-water syrup in which we stewed two fresh pears, perfectly halved. I went directly home from school that day and made pear sauce for our supper. Velma did the same at the Umhoffers, where she worked for room and board. Before the year ended, we had mastered white sauce—thick, thin or medium—mashed potatoes and tomato soup. In the spring, the students invited their mothers to a banquet. A team of girls made tomato soup; another mixed the flour and water for gravy. We all peeled and quartered potatoes to be boiled and mashed. The menu included baked pork chops and Jell-o salad. Velma and I worked efficiently and happily even while cleaning up and washing dishes.

We were much alike, Velma and I. Our early Palmer Method penmanship had taken hold, and our handwriting matched. We wrote and passed notes to each other, sharing secrets about our one great consuming interest—boys. We developed code numbers for our secret loves in case notes fell into the wrong hands.

Together, Velma and I attended the all-high-school Halloween party in the gym. My mother made me a shepherdess costume with a long full skirt—all yellow flowers and sprigs of green on a white background. The white blouse had puffed sleeves, and the black vest laced in front. Papa produced a staff with a crook at the end. Velma wore a three-piece black suit that belonged to a brother. She was so convincing when she came for me that Papa really thought she was a boy. He became excited, called my mother to the front door and said no way was he allowing a thirteen-year old to go to a party with a boy. What a wonderful joke!

At school, the once familiar gym had been transformed. Stumbling down steps, we found a haunted black space—strange corridors of flapping curtains, ghostly voices, occasional screams. Eyes adjusted to the dark, we became aware of white ghost-like figures flitting about and flashes of eerie purple light. Clammy hands guided our fingers to touch the eyes of the dead (peeled grapes) and immersed them in blood (tepid water). After the spook show, the lights came up; we bobbed for apples, sang and enjoyed folk dances.

Toward the end of that party, flushed and hot, I felt a strange wetness and knew for the first time warm blood between my legs. The trauma of the onset of menstruation, so common in feminist literature, was not mine. I was excited to have grown old enough to have the "monthlies." Girls referred to it as "the curse," "falling off the roof," or "my cousin is visiting me." I was grown up.

By Christmas, Velma had replaced Janet Storm and

Evelyn Satter at the top of my list of best friends. We whispered in the cloak room before school, translated Latin together, memorized "The moon was a ghostly galleon . . ." and passed harsh as well as kind judgment on our classmates. Together we despaired of our secret loves ever taking notice of us and comforted each other with a phrase we had read:

> Somewhere the sun is shining
> Somewhere laughing children are at play

*　　*　　*

A town kid, unrelated to any farmers in the community, I knew nothing of farm life. Going home for the weekend with Velma was a big treat for me. Ade (Adolph), a senior in high school and three years older than Velma and youngest of her four brothers, drove us home to the farm the first time I visited there. Four miles on gravel roads in his Model T Ford, and then up the tree-shaded lane to the big two-story farmhouse. Chickens ran about the yard and nasturtiums grew outside the screen door to the kitchen—the heart of the house.

In that room stood the largest square table I had ever seen. Enough sturdy chairs ringed it that anyone and everyone who came in could sit right down. Newspapers and magazines lay on the oilcloth table cover.

A black and brown telephone hung on the wall rang as we came in. Nobody bothered to answer it; four rings meant the call was for a neighbor. Since Velma and I had just arrived, nobody wa interested in listening in on that conversation.

Wiping her hands on her Mother Hubbard apron, Ma Bolte stood in the middle of the room. A raw-boned woman with ample breasts and hips, her white hair was knotted at the back, pulled back tightly. She greeted me with confident enthusiasm. I felt immediately at home.

I was less at ease with Velma's four virile brothers. They seemed to fill the space with loud voices, long arms and legs. I was overwhelmed as well as excited by all that masculinity. But Velma hustled me up the stairs to show me her room. I looked at the books on her shelf, the pictures of movie stars pinned on the walls, and her scrapbooks.

For our supper, Ma Bolte had a crock of potatoes, peeled and sliced soaking in cold water, ready for frying. Raw fried potatoes, crisp bacon and scrambled eggs served with stewed tomatoes and thick slices of fresh bread was very different from the supper snack I was used to at home.

Strong, silent Pa Bolte, one of the area's most prosperous farmers, raised and sold feed cattle, kept dairy cows for milk, and farmed 320 acres of grains and corn. I knew from Papa that Fred Bolte, Sr. was a shrewd dealer on the grain and commodities market. The four big boys talked about the price of hogs, weather reports on the radio and the day's price for a bushel of corn or oats. They talked of silage and other matters completely foreign to me. Profitable farming, I gathered, was sharp mental reckoning as well as hard work.

At one corner of the table next to Ma Bolte, sat her white-haired and wrinkled father-in-law, Grandpa Bolte. Not one word came from his lips; sometimes he spilled his food. Velma was embarrassed, her mother patient.

After supper, Velma and I washed and dried the dishes. My, how many there were! Then we set the table for breakfast and walked about outdoors. Big barns, the sweet smell of clean hay, plump brown-and-white cattle. At dark, we took the Hershey bars Ma Bolte gave us and went up to Velma's room. In her big, double bed, under a patchwork quilt tied with red and yellow yarn knots, we giggled and talked far into the night.

The chicken and egg business formed Ma Bolte's domain. In the morning, Velma and I looked for eggs. We found them in the strangest places—hidden in corners of a cow's stall, under a crooked board leaning against the wall, sometimes right out in the open in front of our eyes. I watched big brother Bill milk the cows; he let me sit on his small, wooden stool. I know now, as I write, the feel of the udders under my fingers and my frustration at not seeing the milk squirt-plop-squirt-plink into the metal pail. Bill laughed at me and made fun of my town dumbness.

I met Velma's family; she met mine. We vowed eternal friendship. We were staunch Emersonians: Man is the Master of his Fate and you can have anything you want if you want it badly enough. We were the laughing children at play.

* * *

Miss Ione Russ taught freshman Latin as well as English. From Blue Earth, a neighboring southern Minnesota town, she was a University of Minnesota graduate in her first teaching position. I always tended to love my teachers, but no one had ever been quite so admired, so adored as she. Her glossy black hair was stylishly done, and she wore fashionable clothes. Even a racoon coat like the ones John Held Jr. sketched in *College Humor* magazine. No saddle shoes for her—stylish Cuban heels that came down the halls with a staccato click I learned to recognize and love. Best of all, I loved her voice— throaty, low, full-bodied—that *declared* with certainty.

She taught us Latin, drew a clear foundation in it for our language so that meanings and spellings emerged logical and clear. She tolerated no sloppy sentences, dangling modifiers or undotted i's. For her I wanted every paper, homework assignment, and test to be perfect.

I became obsessed with vocabulary. The weather was no longer cold but rather *inclement or pitiless*. Instead of seeing a bunch of kids, I saw a *galaxy* of kids. And one day, when Miss Russ came to school in a new black, orange and white dress, all modernistic triangles, dots, and dashes, I told her I loved her dress and found it *eccentric*.

After school, Miss Russ made herself available to her students. She helped with difficult translations or the reworking of a theme, but mostly she seemed to be there to talk. She encouraged me in reading poetry, especially Emily Dickinson, pointed out metaphors and symbols and how they worked in a poem. She coached me in a dramatic art piece I memorized for the declamatory contests and listened sympathetically when I confided my unrequited passion of Bud Johnson. Sometimes she talked with me about her experiences at the university, about her sorority and what good times lay before me when I went to college. We talked about the big world "out there." She made me feel that she believed in me and that I could do anything I wanted if I put my mind to it.

I was not the only student who gravitated to Miss Russ' classroom after school. That sophomores, juniors and seniors, boys as well as girls found those sessions fun made them no less interesting to me. Sometimes that sophomore, Bud Johnson, star of the basketball team, was there too.

It was 1927. In my small world, walking the three blocks home from school in the twilight, my tall shadow stretching far ahead of me, all was right with the world.

11.

Removing the Lenses

I take off the Panglossian lenses. I need not be consistent. I try to be honest. Memories stew, boil and bubble.

*   *   *

During my junior year, Evelyn Satter fell in love with a senior from another town. This left Bud Johnson, my secret love since the seventh grade, on the loose. I seem to have repressed how I made it so, but, before long, he was my boyfriend. Velma was dating Bob, her idol from freshman year. Our romantic daydreams had come true. "Everything comes if a girl will only wait" became established as an absolute. Bud was the star of the basketball team, a gregarious soul, the center of fun activities, and I was walking on clouds. I was sure I had never been so happy.

The year was 1929, four years before Prohibition was repealed. Slow as our development was in comparison with today's youth, we did experiment with alcohol. Parked behind the Tri-Mont Creamery, one of the boys would come up with a flask of pure alcohol. With it we "spiked" near beer. Only the inexperienced did not know enough to shake or mix it up, and, if you didn't—wow, what a taste! Mouth and throat on fire. Potent stuff, but I had never run into trouble . . . until the night of the Ormsby dance. (Into the froth of happy bubbles of memory, a shame foams briskly.) I got drunk.

Those were Big Band days. Husko Hare, Eddie Duchin, and other big name bands came to relatively small towns to play in large halls with crystal balls that hung from the ceiling and filled the space with dancing rainbows. Big live orchestras. Hot jazz. Perhaps because of the strict religious mores at that time, few dances were held in our towns. Ormsby, a short distance to the north, seemed more open. On Friday nights we went to dance there. Before the dance and at intermission, glass bottles of spiked beer hidden in our cars provided refreshment.

On the night in my memory, we had a beer or two before we went in, then danced every dance until intermission when we escaped for the cool outdoors, drank more spiked beer and smoked cigarettes. How grown up and sophisticated. What fun! More dancing until the orchestra played "Good Night, Ladies, Good Night," and we sadly left the hall. We had more spiked beer, and then my world swam in circles. I wanted to go to sleep. The feeling was not pleasant. But there, on either side of me were my two loves, Velma and Bud, insisting that I stand up and keep on walking. They did a good job taking care of me as I staggered in my almost-high heels along the gravel country roads.

Bud gave me his large pocket handkerchief when I threw up. The night was icy, but they walked me and walked me until I was sober enough to be taken home. I managed to get to bed without waking my parents. The handkerchief, a symbol of Bud's caring for me, became a cherished possession. Stained with vomit, I hid it in the green and orange wooden chest that contained my diaries, secret notes, and letters.

I was not convinced, perhaps, that drinking was wrong, but I knew that getting drunk certainly was . . . maybe even a sin.

*   *   *

I have sometimes said that the Great Depression did not really touch me until I left home in 1931. But knowledge of it was there and, had I paid attention, close to the surface.

Papa sometimes played the stock market and rather shrewdly I suspect. Occasional killings brought glorious results. A buying trip to the Cities meant family luxuries as well as dry goods for the store—our first automobile, the Dodge; the rowboat; special vacations to Potato Lake or Duluth; a fur coat for Mother.

But in 1929 the stock market crashed, and the Monterey People's State Bank closed. Papa lost all the money saved to send Ruth and me to the University of Minnesota. He lost his credit rating. Dry goods and groceries came C.O.D. Papa and Uncle Oscar (the Westerdahls had moved to Slayton, Minnesota, where Oscar owned a hardware store) carried on a fancy financial arrangement kiting checks, depositing them in the Slayton and Triumph banks, thus giving each other a few days to collect bills, sell a few more groceries or screwdrivers. Papa once borrowed $1,000 from Martha, our clerk in the store. Imagine the humiliation, the desperation!

Papa and Mother did not discuss money in front of my sister and me, but we knew when they worried. After Ruth and I had left the dinner table and our parents drank their coffee, we heard them talking in low voices, wondering how bills would be paid. One time I heard Papa ask Mother if she thought her friend Mrs. Miller would loan him some money.

Because he could not pay her salary, Papa let Ida go. There was no question of loyal Martha's leaving. She worked for over a year without any salary at all.

With Ida gone, mother spent more time in the store; during summers Ruth and I worked. We were all organized. I even had regular days off. On Saturday night, I took a quarter from the brass National Cash Register, left a note reading, "Wages—Edith, 25 cents," and went down the street to the hotel for a cherry coke.

*   *   *

Velma and I tied for valedictorian. Our grades had been averaged four times, but we were tied to a tenth of a point.

We tossed a coin for the honor. Velma would deliver the salutatorian speech, I the valedictory. I am and always was competitive, but I believe in my heart that Velma never competed with me for grades.

Of the commencement and the speech I gave, I have no recollection. I'm sure it was sentimental, filled with platitudes about the great work waiting for us and our responsibility to do the best for the world and ourselves, to be a credit to good ol' Tri-mont High. We were to work and be responsible. Success would be ours! Laced throughout would have been Horatio Alger, Ralph Waldo Emerson and Mary Baker Eddy.

Disregarding the scholarship to Gustavus Adolphus College, I decided to enter the University of Minnesota the next fall. Velma was headed for Mankato Business College.

Part IV

Edith, age seventeen, at the University of Minnesota.

12.

The University

I have neither diaries nor clear memories of the summer following my high school graduation. Knowing myself, I suspect I drowned in nostalgia one week, looked forward to college the next. For as long as I could remember, my parents had assumed that I would attend the University of Minnesota; I never for a minute considered accepting the scholarship to Gustavus. And, after eleven years of being an A plus student even if it was as a big frog in a small puddle, I had no reason to believe that I would not fit in. Theoretically, I should take the University of Minnesota by storm. I had already been exempted from freshman English.

Mother and I shopped for my college wardrobe: a silky brown velvet coat (an evening wrap) banded at the bottom with a six-inch flare, high-heeled brown pumps and brown and white saddle shoes. A yellow flannel I had worn in high school would do for warm fall days, and the old dark brown cloth (niggerhead, as it was called then) coat would complete the wardrobe.

On a warm September day, my parents delivered me to 1107 Fourth Street S.E., Sarset's rooming house for girls. This three-story, grey-clapboard house would be my new home. Mrs. Sarset's face, all smiles and warm welcome, topped a large-bosomed, solid, overweight body. Mother must have felt happy and confident leaving me in such hands.

The first floor of this house had the Sarset family rooms as well as a living room that served as a gathering place for the roomers. An old upright piano with stacks of sheet music encouraged singing and even dancing. For those who could afford it and signed up in advance, Mother Sarset served dinner one night a week in the dining room.

The second and third floors housed thirteen young women (girls we were then and so I think of us), including the two Sarset daughters, Jo and Margaret. One bathroom served us all, a heavy white canvas curtain separating tub from toilet. A telephone at the foot of the stairway between second and third floor carried a warning handwritten in blue ink: "Ten minute limit. Remember, someone may be dying!"

Up the stairs to the third floor, Mrs. Sarset led me to the room I would share with Helen Skjod, a senior in the business school. My bed, tucked under a sloping ceiling, had a dull brown blanket, and the space beside the bed toward the clothes closet defined my section of the room. I had a window facing east and a desk on the north wall.

If I was anxious or apprehensive, I don't remember. I don't even remember saying good-bye to my parents. I hung up my clothes and began to unpack my new blue suitcase, carefully arranging my hairbrushes, pictures of parents, Ruth, Velma and, of course, Bud on the top of my dresser. I put away my underwear—garter belts, the stiff, hard girdles we wore in 1931, and silk stockings (before nylon). But, finished with all this, I sat down on my newly made-up bed to wait. I didn't know what was next.

My roommate Helen showed up, cheerful and friendly. I was prepared to like her. From my five-foot two and three quarters inches, I looked down at a small-boned, narrow-faced woman with pale blue eyes and short legs. She moved swiftly and surely, reminding me sometimes of a rabbit, sometimes of a little chicken.

Helen asked me to join her for dinner. I accepted with great glee. Things were moving along all right. Over the meal in a small, inexpensive restaurant on Fourth Street, I learned that Helen came from Braham, a small Minnesota town north of Minneapolis. A business degree had always been her goal; having mastered typing and Gregg shorthand, she was well on her way to becoming a model mid-1930s secretary.

Helen walked with me to campus the next morning and steered me to the Administration Building. Then followed the endless matriculation lines, the anxiety of finding the proper buildings, and the scared feeling of standing with hundreds of other anxious freshmen. I shook during the Health Service examination. My Christian Science background was poor preparation for anything having to do with doctors. I had never had a vaccination or injection of any kind. The session with my academic advisor was easier.

On my way home at the end of that long day, I stopped at The Bridge, a restaurant on the corner of Fifteenth and Fourth Streets, to eat a vegetarian plate special. This was to become a popular evening meal—not for the cottage cheese and the healthy vegetables but because of its cheap price and the bran muffin.

When I returned to Sarset House, more girls had moved in; some clustered around the piano. I was the youngest girl in the house, one of two freshman. Seven of us roomed on the third floor, six on the second.

It seemed I never spent time in this house talking about the anxieties or concerns common to first-year students. Today I know that boys and girls from small towns and farms often found the university too much and went home. I never once considered leaving. I wrote letters to my parents, to Bud in Mason City and very long, sometimes daily letters to Velma.

My grandmother's house was a refuge. On many weekends I packed my suitcase and took the streetcar to St. Louis Park. Grandma did not have a telephone, but I was free to show up any time, unannounced, and was welcomed with joy. Mormor and Forfor couldn't do enough for me—mostly feed me. I ate greedily of the Swedish cooking—boiled potatoes and pot roast, sausages, ham and eggs, slice after slice of home-baked bread thick with yellow butter. Listening to their radio was a treat.

And, of course, my childhood friend, Evelyn Dickinson, lived close to Mormor's house. They did have a telephone and I was always welcome there—to play cards or word games, eat some more, and play the role of the important university student. I often spent the night. Evelyn had a ready ear, so when evenings at Sarset's grew unbearably long or lonely, I telephoned her. Limited by the warning on the Sarset phone, I talked ten minutes with her, then waited for her to call me back.

Those visits to St. Louis Park were especially important during fall quarter. They helped me spell the time until Christmas. And I counted the days! Just before the holidays, I stayed up all night studying for exams, and I felt keenly disappointed that my mother did not express concern over the dark circles under my eyes when my parents came to drive me home for Christmas.

We did all the traditional Christmas things: We rolled mustard seed with the heavy steel ball from Sweden, using the spice in the cream gravy with the lutefisk. On Christmas Eve we had pickled beets, *Sylta*, and lutefisk with boiled potatoes, meatballs and rice pudding. It felt wonderful to be home with the people I loved, decorating the Christmas tree with the familiar ornaments. But after we had opened our presents, I said to Ruthie, "Remember when we were little children? Remember how we used to get everything we asked for?"

"Seems like we didn't get so very much," said Ruthie.

"This year seems different . . ."

"Do you think it's 'cuz we're growing up?"

Talk of money dominated the conversations that year. Our parents were forced to meet the growing hardships of the Great Depression. I had been "out of it" for months and had not even read the newspapers—current events and all. One night, sitting on our piano bench, I asked, "Tell me, please, who is this guy Dillinger that everyone is talking about?" My mother was aghast. What kind of school allowed such seclusion from the world?

That holiday season had some disappointments too. Most of Velma's short holiday from business school was spent at her parents' farm. Bud stayed in Mason City. No

New Year's dance had been planned, and even if one had, I had no date. Social events were limited to time with my parents' friends. And I spent a couple of days miserable with the flu. Then too, I weighed 135 pounds, making food hardly a comfortable or acceptable solace. Eager as I had been to come home, I was quite ready to go back for winter quarter.

*   *   *

Blocking, burying or hiding disappointments and unfulfilled expectations did not make them go away. Despite my prolific letter writing, my Christian Science attitude that all was well, and my optimistic nature, I was not always happy. Careful effort and some pain uncover memories of homesickness that drove me to snuggle into my pink comforter where I cried myself to sleep. I had known separation from my parents before: camp, staying at the Westerdahls or Mormor's. But this was different. Nobody really knew me, and the desire to be with my mother and father and sister, the need for the familiar, the desire for home often overwhelmed me. I wanted cocoa and toast at Mother's kitchen table. I would have given anything just to see the scrawny geraniums Mother insisted on harboring over winter on the sill of the south window in my bedroom.

Watching the freshman girls who had come from Minneapolis West High School swish about in their pleated skirts and bright jackets, I quickly learned that my wardrobe was not exactly right. Indeed, I felt that everything about me was wrong. Those oh-so confident, self-assured girls, the privileged class, shook their heads so their hair flew; they laughed and joked, knew their way around, and flirted with all the cute boys. I tried to tell myself that I wanted to be serious, that I *was* serious; I told myself that those girls were smug and superficial. But I had no defense against them. I, who had been a big frog in a small puddle, was reduced to a dull cabbage, maybe a Brussels sprout.

French class seemed to accentuate my difference from the West High girls. Many of those students had had some high school French; I was not doing well. One day the instructor suggested that I learn *Je ne sais pas* and keep it at the tip of my tongue. The embarrassment of being criticized in front of the class hung with me for weeks. Freudianly, I lost my French book by *accident* just before the winter quarter exam. My low C was nothing to be happy about.

Encouraged by the French instructor in an attempt to achieve a hold on academic social society, I joined the French Club. I will never forget the below zero January night of the French Dance. Mustering all possible courage, standing tall and smiling all the while, I walked from Sarset's to what is now Burton Hall. In a large hall, the members of French Club from many classes danced to a lively five-piece orchestra. I was not the only student who came alone, but I might as well have been. By 11:30 or midnight, no one had asked me to dance. Mortified, in below zero weather, I walked across campus in my brown niggerhead coat, tears streaming down my fat cheeks.

*   *   *

Bud came to visit me. I had mooned over him in my grammar school years, dated him since my junior year in high school and missed him acutely after he went off to Mason City, Iowa, to make his fortune. He had a sister in Minneapolis and called one day to say he had his sister's car and would pick me up at seven. I dressed with care and apprehension. The sober countenance of my face in the mirror did not quite fit the high school cheer leader that was Bud's best girl.

When Bud arrived, he looked smaller than the outstanding athlete I remembered. I felt stiff and strange, almost numb, as we walked to the black coupe. He talked rapidly. He had come, he said, to ask me to marry him. Knowing my parents would not approve, he wanted me to elope with him that very minute, saying that the money he made as a truck driver would be plenty for our livelihood.

I have often asked myself what kept me from that dramatic elopement. I know I felt the presence of my parents. I could never do that to them. And, although my expectations of the glamour and excitement of university life hardly had been fulfilled, I was not ready for a quick way out. I had not

even come close to admitting disappointment or homesickness. But, there was something more. All the night conversations with the girls at Sarset's, all the books I had read,
the dreams of my future—all had convinced me that boys
did not necessarily rank top priority. The intellectual life
mattered more.

Bud was disappointed, but he seemed to take my refusal
well. He wanted to take me to the Marigold Ballroom, but I
didn't want to tell the girls at Sarset's that while Margaret
Sarset was dancing at the St. Paul Hotel, I was at the Marigold.
What a snob! Instead we went to see *The Champ* with Wallace
Beery and Mickey Rooney at the fanciest movie house in
downtown Minneapolis. The lobby seemed all red velvet and
gilded crystal chandeliers. A long-haired beauty in miles of
chiffon played a golden harp.

But Bud and I had little to say to each other. We sat
silently in the balcony. After the movie I chattered nervously
about school, the girls at Sarset's, and sorority rush. I was
unhappy for years about my behavior that night and the
disappointment I'm sure I caused Bud.

* * *

And then sorority rush came. Unlike French Club, I felt
comfortable at these teas and dinners. All those knowl-
edgeable, established people were so nice to me.

"Edith, I'd like you to know . . ." and "Edith, may I
present . . ." on and on, all around the large rooms. Clusters
of girls engaged in what was described as "polite and animated conversation." But I felt a part of this. They made me
feel my clothes were right, that they were truly interested
in what I had done in high school, where I lived, and what I
thought of the university.

I balanced tea cups, ate an endless array of cookies and
cakes, wondering how life in a big sorority house would com-
pare to Sarset's.

My older cousin, Big Edith, had pledged Sigma Kappa
and lived at the house for three years. If EK was right for
Big Edith, it would be right for me. I turned down other bids.

* * *

This, then, is the stuff that bubbles to the surface when I think of my freshman year at the university. It seems to have little to do with academic life. Well, I had never found it necessary to study in high school, and I certainly did not learn that at the university in 1931-1932. I attended classes, read the material and took notes in classes, but I never mastered the art of studying. Except for Sophomore Comp, all my classes were very large, and I think I may have enjoyed that anonymity.

I had never written a high school paper that had not merited an "A" and high praise from my teachers. That made the "F" on my first Sophomore Comp paper somewhat disheartening to say the least. I don't remember the specific criticisms, but whatever the professor said must have taken hold, for I earned an "A" in the course.

I remember spending hours in the library developing a bibliography of poetry that had to do with death—index cards full, piles of them. When I carried some of that poetry to St. Louis Park for a weekend with the Dickinsons, Bruce asked, "Do you understand this stuff?"

"Well, uh, no, not exactly," I admitted, "but I like the sound of it."

Pretty thin . . . those memories of the intellectual life.

On a hot, windy day in late spring, I packed my suitcase, rolled up my quilt and left Sarset's, the end of my freshman year. I said a tearful good-bye to all my friends, fully expecting to see them the next fall. And so, back to Triumph. . . .

13.

In Limbo

By the fall of 1932, the full impact of the Great Depression had filtered down to all sections of the country, and the farming community of Martin County was definitely depressed. Return to campus for my sophomore year was out of the question. Papa, with his usual optimism, felt certain that if I would stay home and work in the store that one year, he would recoup, and I would be back at the university the following year.

I countered keen disappointment with an enthusiastic commitment to work. I would consider it a real job. Work, any work, was considered good in 1932. I would help Papa, and, who knew, maybe merchandising would prove just right for me. Maybe one day I would own a great merchandising business.

So I spent that year working in the store. I worked behind the counter, sacked prunes in brown paper bags, ground coffee, matched thread to lengths of percale, helped farmers try on heavy work shoes, and "candled" eggs in the back room. I helped set up displays and was very pleasant to all the customers. I went on buying trips to the Cities with Papa and worked with him on specials, folding and addressing circulars he cranked off on the mimeograph.

And I liked being with my parents and my sister. Being home felt comfortable. We all liked each other, and Mother and Papa were both good-natured optimists who never complained about work. A life so integrated upstairs (home) and downstairs (the store) never led me to regard work as something undesirable.

By spring, however, it was evident that neither my energy nor Papa's attempt to update his merchandising methods had greatly affected our profit figures. During the summer Ruth also helped in the store. We were no longer proud of being there, and when someone came in who had been away to college, we felt like hiding behind the counter . . . once we did.

I felt I had wasted my time. Skipping a year of college was not in my plans, nor in my mother's plans for her daughter. She talked often of her daughters getting out of that small town. I suspect she had a dreadful fear that either or both of us might fall in love with and marry one of the country boys around us and end up living on a farm. Although she had settled in Triumph, she never felt rooted and didn't want her children to stay there.

I felt as if I were in limbo. Old women now, my sister and I talk about that time. We smile with love and sympathy for the girls we were. Ruth says, "It really bugged me that everyone thought you were so smart. I was valedictorian of my class, too!"

I tell her I envied her because she had not had to wear glasses, because our parents' friends seemed to like her better than they liked me, and because she never got too fat. She was popular with the boys. Today, Ruth and I agree. I was not in limbo. But all the pieces of the mosaic fit together. We needed to be in that place at that time for our lives to pivot in just the way they did.

*   *   *

Late in the summer, Mrs. Dickinson wrote to suggest that I stay with them and enroll in school fall quarter. Papa agreed. He would be happy to bring groceries to the Dickinson house every time he made a trip to the cities. Papa also gave Evelyn a violin I had never heard him play. The Dickinsons even arranged transportation to campus for me with Bruce's friends.

But during the first two months of school, I realized how difficult it must be for Papa to find the money for my tuition and books. The idea of working, earning money to support myself and relieve my parents, loomed large. Maybe I could even help them. Ruthie would have to have some education the next year.

I cancelled out of the university and enrolled in Calhoun Business School, on the second floor of a building on Lagoon and Hennepin, a familiar neighborhood. My goal was to learn to type and take shorthand—skills that would enable me to support myself and maybe help my family.

In 1933 the machines to be mastered included manual Royal and L.C. Smith typewriters, Friden calculators, and Burroughs adding machines. I would have to master typing, Gregg shorthand, bookkeeping and spelling for my secretarial certificate. To the tune of phonograph records, I typed:

a;sldkfjghfjdksla;
A sly brown fox quickly jumped over the lazy dog.
Now is the time for all good men to come to the aid of their party.

A more boring, tedious process I cannot imagine. But I was highly motivated, kept at it and did well. I enjoyed learning the art of Gregg's squiggles, lines, and curves. I was good at that, too, and even today find myself mentally taking notes in Gregg. My arithmetic was adequate, but I found bookkeeping an utter bore, did not work hard and knew no satisfaction in the exercises. That I was in a spelling class struck me as ludicrous. Imagine, then, my embarrassment when, in a class exercise on answering the phone and spelling, I said, "K as in cat."

By the time the winter snows melted and Chapman Graham (a sweets shop on the main floor of our building) displayed chocolate rabbits and pastel-colored eggs, I was pretty sick of the Calhoun Business School. The classrooms were noisy with the clatter of typewriters and adding machines, the air stuffy with the smell of old varnish, papers, cigarette smoke, dust. . . . My mind was dusty, too. I ate too much chow mein at the Port Arthur restaurant each noon and wandered aimlessly along the avenues on sunny afternoons. Sometimes I attended matinees in the Lagoon Theater. I once ate fifty cents worth (the whole bag!) of Fanny Farmer chocolate-covered almonds in the safe womb of the movie house.

I had had it. I really had. So what if I didn't have the diploma or certificate and had not finished the bookkeeping course? I had achieved the sixty-five words per minute speed on the typewriter, knew how to set up a good business letter and had the Gregg down pat. I was ready to go to work.

* * *

My first real job was in Fairmont. It was 1934, and I felt lucky to have work that paid forty-five dollars a month. I also was about to move in with Velma, who was working in Fairmont. In the office of the Fairmont Production Credit Association, I answered the phone, kept books, took short-hand and transcribed it into neat letters well-spaced on the page. I took pride in those letters and my balanced books. I searched Court House records and typed abstracts. I not only cleaned and polished the desk of my overfed, bald-headed, pasty-faced boss, I cleaned and polished his ashtrays and his eye glasses. Every other day he bought me a Coke; the alternate days I bought him one. When I refused to sleep with him, he did not fire me—my work was too good. (One night I worked until 11:00 to find a five-cent error in my books—found it too!) I overheard him tell a salesman, "What do I care if I can't make her? She's nothing but a fat-faced little Swede."

God, how I hated that man! My mother used to make pie crust by cutting lard into flour with two pastry knives. One night I dreamed that, holding a razor blade in each hand, I cut his bald head, producing a sharp pattern of Vs and Xs in his scalp. It never occurred to me to leave.

14.

My Marjorie Morningstar Story

I sit here remembering. Waiting. How many women have waited how many hours for a telephone to ring? Angry women, angry because of the power a man can have—angry women, forgetting that women have that power over men too. But that's not what I was remembering.

I was remembering waiting for a phone call from M.O. Terry when Velma and I lived together in a second-story rented room with the Roethke family in Fairmont, Minnesota. This was my *Marjorie Morningstar* (a Herman Wouck novel) period of my life, and, although I might laugh now that I am an old woman, it is not an amused laugh, for I remember that love with joy and anguish.

I was twenty. Velma and I worked as secretaries in that southern Minnesota town of five thousand souls, she for the phone company, I with Fairmont Production Credit. We ate dinner out each evening, most often at Gus Boosalis' Sweet Shop. That was the first year I drank coffee. M.O. Terry also ate dinner each night at Gus'.

M.O. used to look at me and smile. Then he took to telephoning and asking me out. He was in his forties, an executive at Raukway Motors, the largest industry in town. I laughed and made fun of him, calling him "that old man."

One Thursday he called to invite me to a duck dinner at the Fairmont Hotel. He had been hunting, and the hotel was to roast the ducks and put on a fancy dinner for him and his friends. I had nothing to do and was interested in the dinner, in having a Saturday night date, interested also because Chuck Meister and his beautiful girl friend would be there. I relished the idea of getting all dressed up in my black satin dress with rhinestone buttons.

The evening began with cocktails at M.O.'s cabin on the lake. The word "cocktail" comes easily now that I am in my sixties, many cocktails older. But that evening at M.O.'s cabin, I had my first martini. M.O. introduced me to the drama of the martini with the words, "A martini, an olive, and a kiss from you. This, my sweet, is heaven." How could I not be charmed and fall madly in love? Chuck was not even in M.O.'s class!

Over six feet tall, not ugly, not handsome—a Walter Matthau type—M.O. had an athletic body, very strong, and was a dreamy dancer. He called me his "dear little pushkin," a word he said was Russian for "little girl." His eyes twinkled, his laugh was uproaringly infectious. His strong arms held me tight. That he was twenty years my senior seemed utterly insignificant to me.

The affair lasted something over a year. We danced a lot, barbecued thick steaks over many fires, went to movies, played cards. We spent many evenings at the cabin at the lake. I had read my Hemingway, and I was in love. The earth moved. And I waited. Waited for phone calls, waited for him to come at the appointed hour, waited for him to ask me to marry him.

We drove to Minneapolis for a football game, and I sat through the entire game seeing little because I was too vain to wear my glasses. Dinner was elegant at Bergsings' Restaurant, where the waiters wore tuxedos. On New Year's Eve, we saw a Lily Pons movie. He professed much knowledge of music; I had none. The night was icy, and I remember brilliant stars—in the sky and, surely, in my eyes as well.

That spring he told me he could not marry me. I sat beside him in his car. "If only I were younger," he said, "I'd know exactly where my happiness lies. But I love you too much—far too much to ruin your life. When I am sixty, you'll be forty. The difference is too great. I am sad. . . ."

So, I waited in vain for the phone to ring. I knew I would never recover. Velma tried to reason with me, saying, "He's an old man. You're out of your mind." I serenely proclaimed, "M.O. is a complement to God." I quit my job and left town. Perhaps in another location, I might recover.

Later, I learned that M.O. had married. Oh, yes, I was too young. He would not ruin my life. But he married Meg, a teacher (a position with more status than a secretary in Fairmont in the 1930s), sister to a famous movie star. I was too young, but Meg was only six months older than I. Meg was beautiful, clever, fun, poised, and self-confident. Nothing could throw her. She baked a birthday cake for M.O. when they were first married and burned it black. She decorated it with a black ribbon and used it for a centerpiece. Everyone loved her.

Part V

Edith, age twenty-six.

15.

White Gardenias

He brought me gardenias. The sweet smell of the white gardenia. The whitest whites are hard, like bright enamel, but the white of mine was soft, like velvet. I wore a long black taffeta dress and a full, black velvet coat. My hair was drawn back in the Russian countess look. We went dancing . . . Easter time in Triumph. He brought white gardenias for my mother, my sister and me. No gardenias in the southern Minnesota town where I grew up, but we had real gardenias growing on live bushes when he took me south for our honeymoon. Soft, pure, uncluttered, sensuous . . . the memory of falling in love with my husband.

My marriage has survived more than forty years. Paul and I have raised twn daughters, known four grandchildren—two boys and two girls. Symmetrical, orderly. Yes, Dr. Jung, in forty years there are reactions and transformations. Experience, aging, growth.

Who can know another? Am I not a different Edith to each person who knows me? And what does it mean "to know"? Our progeny can never know Paul Mucke as I first knew him, know him as I have known him. Family centered, loyal, steadfast, principaled, a man of strong character, but mortal, so not perfect. But oh, a *good* man. No, there is no way to know, but I can try. . . .

*   *   *

I was the secretary. He was my boss.

The week between Christmas and New Year's, 1935. A period of slow economic recovery following the Great Depression. Twenty-one years old, my insides sinking— scared, I sat beside the desk of G.S. Webster, office manager of Gamble-Skogmo, Inc. and Gamble Stores, in Minneapolis. No, he said, they were not hiring at present, but what were my interests, what department would I choose in which to work, and just what were my experiences—in my own words.

I talked: the year at the university, secretarial school and work at the Production Credit Association and legal work in Fairmont. He had heard of the town. He must have sized me up as a "young girl from outstate come to the big city of Minneapolis." I told him I liked working with people. He listened. And then he told me I could come to work in the typing department.

How happy I was! I was in the city, about to start a job paying sixty dollars a month and invited again to live with my longtime friend Velma who had gone to work at Gamble's a few months earlier. The two of us still quoted the Arabic lines we had long since taken as our theme:

> Open Tents, Open Hearts
> Let the winds blow
> Let love come in

In the mid-1930s long before Xerox machines stood in every corner drug store, before computers and complex communication devices, large companies had pools of typists. At Gambles on North Third Street in the warehouse district of Minneapolis, the smell of Atwood's coffee roasting filled the air, and the typing department was housed in a spacious room with glaring fluorescent lights on the second floor. The building had once been a warehouse. Young women sat with dictaphone equipment attached to their ears, their fingers pounding rapidly on nonelectric typewriters. Others

Paul T. Mucke, age thirty-seven.

of us, more fortunate, we thought, transcribed squiggles and lines and circles of Gregg from our steno notebooks.

Shortly after I was admitted to the secretarial pool, I was sent downstairs to the Executive Offices to take dictation from Paul T. Mucke, Assistant Secretary-Treasurer and Comptroller of Gamble-Skogmo, Inc. I wore a brown crepe dress with a white satin collar and high-heeled brown pumps. I suspect I did not put my glasses in front of my near-sighted eyes until I had seated myself beside his desk and taken out my notebook.

Oh my, I did like the looks of him. I liked his deep, strong voice, his slow and deliberate word choice, his clear enunciation and explicit instructions as to periods and paragraphs. Here was a man who knew and understood what it was all about. Looking up from my notebook, waiting for the next words, I saw an unfurrowed forehead, prominent, round, blue-grey eyes, full lips in a square face, a strong jaw, and tanned skin. Sturdy German stock, I thought, that solid, loyal, you-can-depend-on-them type. From that first trip downstairs, I was aware of powerful chemistry brewing.

If, as William James wrote, mortals are born either optimists or pessimists, perhaps it is also true that we are born romantics or realists. English and French novels had nurtured the romantic in me. Maybe I was ready and waiting for just such attraction. In the late 1930s, it was still possible for a twenty-one-year-old to hang onto the romantic notion that there would be a Mr. Right.

And could that feeling elicit a response by its existence? Or was I responding to something in Paul? Within a week, Paul had talked with the office manager, and word came down that Edith Johnson was to be assigned to do all Paul Mucke's work and would not be asked to do any other miscellaneous work in the typing department. Paul's previous secretary had been promoted to Assistant Office Manager. I didn't know it, but I had been on trial and passed the grade.

Well into this work and this chemistry process, I was shocked to hear from a dictaphone operator that Paul was married. My first reaction was that it had to be a mistake. When I learned that he had been separated from his wife for some time, I felt better. Then I learned that it had been a Catholic marriage, and I again felt worse.

*   *   *

The summer of 1936 was historic for its heat wave. For days the temperature never went below 100 degrees. Velma and I had moved to Lagoon on the Mall, a red-brick, three-story apartment on Humboldt Avenue South; the sun beat mercilessly on the flat roof of our top floor apartment on the south side of the building. I remember getting off the yellow streetcar with the woven cane seats, imprints of the weave on the back of our dresses, the super-heated air at pavement level hitting us in the face; we were almost paralyzed by the heat. One evening we filled the bath tub with cold water, set our supper on a chair next to the tub and, both of us sitting in the cold water, dined on milk, radishes, bread and butter. Cool comfort while it lasted.

No fans, no air conditioning. Sleep was out of the question in the oppressive heat. Sometimes we spent most of the night lying on the shore of Lake Calhoun after our evening swim. We were not alone; half of Minneapolis seemed to sleep out of doors that summer.

We wore girdles in those days before panty hose, and slips. Standard practice in the heat: at morning break we removed our girdles and rolled our hose; at noon our hose came off, and, later, during the afternoon we chucked slips.

The hours I spent sitting beside Paul's desk, taking dictation and learning about the work for which I was responsible, I was oblivious to the heat. Telling myself this was a simple boss-secretary relationship did not dim my curiosity about him. I asked questions with all my nerve ends open. While I sat beside Paul's desk, notebook in hand, he sometimes talked a little about himself.

He had grown up in Fergus Falls, finished high school in three years, and attended Macalaster College on a scholarship. After summer work in a Fergus Falls bank, he did not return to college. I learned he was studying law at the St. Paul College of Law several evenings each week. He had a host of men friends with whom he hunted, fished, and took canoe trips on the Gunflint Trail.

He wore tailored suits; even his shirts were custom made—Evans Tailoring. He bought big white linen handkerchiefs with an old English "M" monogrammed on the corner, and when he walked out of the office in his cocky straw hat, he looked downright jaunty.

Everything I learned about him increased my attraction to him. When he told me about the new Packard he planned to buy—fulfillment of a dream—I dreamed of going riding with him in that luxurious tan car. He bought the car and left with friends for a canoe trip, asking me what I would like him to bring me. Oh, I said jokingly, a small Indian child would be fine. He brought me a tiny beaded Indian doll.

Then, one summer night Paul offered to drive me home in his new Packard sedan.

"I'd offer you a drink," he said, "but it's election day, and the bars are all closed." Then he went on: "But, if you would not be afraid to come to my apartment, I would buy you a drink there."

I agreed.

At his apartment in the Elmhurst on Grant Street, he asked me what I would like to drink. With all the would-be sophistication of my twenty-one years, I said a martini would be nice. We each drank one. Then he kissed me and said, "Oh, I've wanted to do that for a long time."

"Oh," I said, "I've wanted you to do that for a long time."

And that's how it all began.

*   *   *

For four years we continued to work together, seeing a great deal of each other outside the office. We had great fun, and spent money freely. That Paul had been married did not disturb me. He said, "It simply wasn't right—ever, from the beginning—and I left her." Out of consideration for his wife, Anne's parents, he agreed not to be divorced while they were still living. I was glad there were no children. I had complete trust in Paul. I was in love, and the man I loved loved me. Miracle enough.

Most women in those years married in their mid to late twenties. I was young, enjoying life and not eager to change anything. I knew that when Anne got around to wanting a divorce and Paul and I married, I would have to leave my job. Then I wouldn't see him all day! It never occurred to either of us that I might continue to work. Getting married for us meant setting up housekeeping and having children.

We had season tickets to the Minnesota football games and never missed one. We drank Planters Punches at the Commerce Club where the journalists and young lawyers hung out. On Saturday nights we danced to the music of big name bands at the Nicollet, the Radisson and the St. Paul Hotel. We dined and danced at the Covered Wagon, Harry's Cafe or Charlie's Cafe Exceptionale. We listened to piano players until three and four in the morning. Only once did we plan a picnic: food in the car, we drove to Minnetonka, around and around and around. We never found a place that suited Paul, so, finally we had our picnic in his apartment. Because we both liked rare roast beef and Roquefort cheese, it was obvious we were meant for each other. On our first New Year's Eve together, I greeted him at the door in a black taffeta formal and a black velvet evening coat with a white rabbit collar. He handed me a shiny white box. Perched on moist tissues was my first gardenia. I don't remember much of the party or where we went, but the gardenia remains a precious jewel.

I met Paul's sister, Corinne, who also worked at Gambles and was a year older than I, and his parents in Fergus Falls. Mother Mucke was a typical old-fashioned grandmother even before she became one. Nothing gave her more pleasure than to have her children at home. Paul T. Mucke, Senior, postmaster, was a Yankee born in St. Louis. Intelligent, tall, angular and erect, with a halo of white hair, he liked movies and playing cards at the Chippewa Club. I felt his approval and was comfortable with him.

We visited my parents in Triumph, where Paul was accepted and welcomed at our house with the same enthusiasm shown me by his parents. We ate large family dinners, played bridge with my parents, Ruth and her friend Tryg.

The year before we were married, Paul graduated from

the St. Paul College of Law. His purpose had been to learn, and learn he did, graduating top student in his class. Satisfied in his position at Gambles, he saw no reason for changing his work or his location.

Velma was married in August of 1939. Ruth and Tryg married in October. I was maid of honor at her wedding. Living alone in an apartment, I found myself cozy and happy. I remember coming home from work on a hot Saturday and spending all afternoon lying on the floor reading *Anna Karenina*, mindful of the joys inherent in living alone. I read a book by Marjorie Hillis, *Live Alone and Like It*. The last sentence read, "Live alone and like it, and you'll never have to."

* * *

A gentle rain was falling, and the sidewalks were slippery with leaves. On that October evening, Paul came to me with special news: He had received notice that Anne was ready, willing to agree to a divorce. We would be married the following spring, April first. Don and Dottie Miller, our very good friends, suggested that we be married at their home. It would be a small wedding; Don would be best man, my sister, Ruth, matron of honor.

Mid-afternoon on March fifteenth, I said good-bye to Gambles. All the way home on the streetcar, I wept. And when I left my small apartment, I wept. I had been so happy there. I looked forward to a glorious future of making a home, keeping house and raising the children we would have, and I would have hated the idea of continuing to work and interfering with that. I was happy in the knowledge that the man I loved wanted to take over the responsibility for my life—for my dental bills, my glasses, my clothes and food; for me *and* our children, not only for as long as he would live, but for as long as I might live.

The last two weeks of March I spent with my parents in Triumph. I loved that time. Leisurely days and long talks with my mother, sleeping late in the morning, household hints from neighbors as well as my mother, and a shower given by the Triumph Embroidery Club (they gave me a peach-colored chenille bedspread), and then Easter.

Paul came for Easter weekend in the new black Packard coupe that we would drive south for our honeymoon. Ruth and Tryg came from Fairmont. Paul brought gardenia corsages for Ruth and Mother and me. It was a happy time. I remember feeling overwhelmed by my love for Paul, feeling that life was now absolute perfection and the life before me ablaze with beautiful expectations. Surely it was all too good to be true; surely some catastrophe would occur before the great event would come to pass!

April first and all was well. In an upstairs bedroom of my grandmother's house in St. Louis Park, I woke to sunlight streaming through the east windows, streaming upon the bed in which my mother and I slept together the night before my wedding day. The aroma of Swedish meat balls sneaked up the stairway and down the hall. After breakfast, I took the streetcar downtown to have my hair and nails done. At three o'clock, Papa drove Mother and me in his Pontiac coupe to the Miller's house at 4511 Drexel Avenue in Edina.

I weighed 110 pounds on Dottie's bathroom scale before I dressed in the white satin dress that Ruth had worn—soft, white, gardenia-like satin. When Mother had buttoned the thirty-three satin buttons down the back of the dress, straightened the stand-up collar, arranged the sleeves with the long points that stretched over the back of my hands, and distributed the fold of the long train, she put her arms about me and we looked at each other with tear-brimmed eyes. I wore Dottie's veil (something borrowed) and a blue garter. Around my neck I wore the cameo my parents had given me for my high school graduation.

Present were our four parents, Corinne and Velma (both seven or eight months pregnant), their husbands, Ruth and Tryg, the two young Miller daughters, and Don and Dottie. I see mother in bois du rose, Paul's mother in navy. Both pregnant women wore navy and white.

The great moment arrived. To the stains of Rollie Altmeyer's organ music, Ruthie, in rose taffeta, came down the winding staircase and crossed the living room to where Paul, Don and the minister stood. The so-familiar Lohengrin wedding march—I had wanted that. I came down the stairs, walked slowly across the room, the faces of my friends and parents a blur, but Paul looked beautiful in his charcoal grey suit with black-and-white-striped tie. "Dearly beloved, we are gathered here. . ." but with the "in sickness" deleted in deference to my Christian Science belief. I must have said "I do," though I don't remember. And we were wed.

*   *   *

A month later, after our driving tour to Florida and a trip to Havana, we returned to our one-bedroom apartment at 3707 Grand Avenue South. Here I would be a housewife years before that term became "just a housewife." It was a comfortably furnished first-floor apartment. The one piece of furniture we owned, a glass-topped coffee table from Corinne and her husband, graced our living room; the peach chenille spread from the Triumph Embroidery Club covered our bed. Venetian blinds at the windows, plants on the sills.

When Paul left for work the day following our return, I wept. Why had I done this, I asked myself. Before we were married, I could be with him all day. Now I would not see him nearly as much.

A dried gardenia on the closet shelf.

White satin pumps in the basement.

16.

Goodwife

How I loved being a bride and a housekeeper! I was convinced that Paul and I had the world's most perfect marriage. Wasn't I truly in love, and didn't I want to please him more than anything in the whole wide world? I wanted to be the perfect wife—efficient housekeeper, creative homemaker, understanding companion and friend, and passionate lover. I had absorbed enough *Good Housekeeping* and *Ladies Home Journal* articles to understand that I would not be "cleaning up somebody's mess" but rather "preparing a lovely space for someone I loved to come home to."

The minute Paul left for work in the morning, I washed the breakfast dishes and made our bed. Following the example of Gladys Arends, my neighbor across the hall, I scrubbed the bathroom and kitchen floors every day. Light walls, a southern exposure, and wide uncurtained windows made our first floor Grand Avenue apartment a pleasant place. Paul was meticulously neat; I never had to pick up his dirty underwear or socks.

But housekeeping did not fill my days. I bowled one morning a week with friends at a Lake and Hennepin alley and rode the Kenwood Parkway trails on horseback twice a week. I tried out the Shrine Women's Auxiliary, but decided it was not for me.

We had Don and Dottie to dinner, and I often called her on the phone, putting into practice all her cooking and house-keeping hints: Never, never let a waste basket overflow. Snap, don't cut, the stalks of asparagus. Add an egg yolk to white sauce to make it richer and better. Use anything except chives for a centerpiece.

In January, I knew I was pregnant and loved it, gained weight and dismissed a little nausea in the mornings as noth-ing to fuss about. A letter from Ruthie announcing the antic-ipated arrival of "a little stranger" was good news—we would go through our first pregnancies together.

Paul cared tenderly for me and our to-be-born child. Early bedtimes, scheduled walks, evening rides to Abdallah's Ice Cream Store where I licked clean the heavy glass dishes of caramel sundaes. In midsummer, he suggested I might like a holiday before "the time" came upon me. While he tended his office, I rode the train (first class) to visit his mother in Fergus Falls, then on to Graceville to be with Ruth and Tryg. In identical pink and white gingham butcher boy maternity dresses with pink ankle socks to match, Ruth and I walked the streets of Graceville and dusty country roads, ate ice cream cones, ran to the radio every time we heard "Puff the Magic Dragon," and stored up enough joy and laughter to last both of us a lifetime.

When Gladys Arends caught me reading Jan Valtin's *Out of the Night,* she raved—Hitler's atrocities would do neither me nor my unborn child any good! We all talked and read about the war in Europe and Africa, but nothing really penetrated my happiness during those months.

Catherine Elizabeth was born on the fourth of Sep-tember. Paul's mother came to stay with us and pamper me. My mother was in Graceville; Ruthie's baby Roxanne had been born three weeks earlier.

I loved nursing our beautiful, brown-eyed baby with her smooth, golden-tan skin—not pasty white or red like some babies in the nursery. I obeyed the doctor's orders implicitly: a bath in her canvas bathinette each morning, a buggy ride every afternoon for air and sun, and food every four hours (I would let her cry for ten minutes waiting for the clock to give me permission to nurse her).

Paul adored Baby Cathy—changed her diapers, held her when she cried, burped her, and took her for buggy rides on Saturday and Sunday afternoons. The first Christmas, Paul showered us both with gifts—an ice blue satin housecoat and a handmade Yolande nightgown with lace inserts, perfume, fluffy stuffed toys, gaily painted rattles, and Nanette dresses. Paul's child was to be treated as well as Cousin Orv's— "everything on a gold platter."

*　　*　　*

As wonderful as this early time was, I was not blind to some empty spaces in my "perfect" marriage.

I found a place to dump irritations and complaints in what Velma, Corinne and I laughingly called our Sewing Club. The three of us, all in our late twenties with our first babies, got together regularly with our babies for lunch and sometimes, but not often, pushed needle and thread up and down or in and out. Mostly we talked.

"Paul never calls me during the day to see how I am," I told them. "I wonder if he cares. He never asks me what I've done. And he always puts the baby first."

"If my husband comes home one more night," quipped Corinne, "and asks me what I've done all day, I'll hit him over the head."

Velma countered with a story of how her husband, Lou, complained of the noise she made in the kitchen while doing the dishes. Her response was to walk into the living room, stand before him with hands on hips and let him have it. "If you are annoyed when I drop something, just remind yourself that's part of the cost of having me around to clean up!" And that took care of that.

Corinne's husband brought too many people home to dinner. I didn't have enough people coming to dinner. With understanding and laughter, individual problems all turned out to be minor.

*　　*　　*

On December seventh, the Japanese bombed Pearl Harbor, but the war was not a big issue in our lives; nobody thought it would last long. Ruth wrote me of her anxieties concerning Tryg's draft status. His number never came up. Because he had gone to college on R.O.T.C. funds, Corinne's husband had military obligations, but Paul and Lou's ages kept them out. We read the papers, sympathized with women whose husbands or brothers were gone, lamented the fate of the Jewish people and cursed Hitler. But, other than gas rationing (Paul and I bought bicycles), meat and sugar rationing, and margarine that I had to color to look like butter, the personal lives of my immediate family remained untouched. We really didn't go without anything we needed. We listened to the radio and I wrote letters to cousins far away in the Pacific.

But the war kept us from buying a house and even furniture. I have a vivid memory of standing on a plot of land in Sunnyslope, Edina, on Minnehaha Creek. This would be a fine place for a house, we said, and, when the war is over and prices come down, we'll build a house on a lot like this. In the meantime, our baby began walking, then running about, and we wanted a yard. We rented a furnished house at 4709 Bryant Avenue South in 1943. Cathy played in our fenced back yard; Paul mowed the lawn and planted flower seeds, and I cheerfully kept house. When Cathy was two years old, we planned a second child. What luck I had having babies! Ten months later our second child was born.

*   *   *

During the time in that little brown bungalow, I began to acknowledge—not a problem, exactly—but some discontent with my marriage. Paul and I were so different. I saw him as such an introvert who felt all he needed and wanted was Cathy and me. He liked staying home and did not recognize the need I had for evenings out or social life outside the family. About this time we began part of an evening dinner-bridge group. We didn't meet often, but that we met regularly was important to me. Birthdays and anniversaries meant going out to dinner with the Millers. Occasionally dances or parties at the Shrine Club brightened my life. But Paul's lack of enthusiasm for any social event made me uncomfortable—a discomfort that I fought but never conquered.

Before we had married, I knew myself to be social and outgoing and that Paul was more a loner, less interested in others' company, but I had this crazy idea that my all-encompassing love for him was such that I could encourage him to laugh more than he had before, have fun . . . shine.

And, I suppose, I had eaten and digested more than my share of fairy tale romances and knew how to look at life through rose-colored glasses. But, in my loneliness, I began to fear that an appreciation of rare roast beef and Roquefort cheese might not be quite enough. I read an article by a psychiatrist or marriage counselor who wrote that if your husband liked ball games and you liked ballet, never mind. If you had a mortgage, a dining room table, children, and your bed in common, you had a great deal. That reinforced my positive self-talk. We had our marriage, our Cathy, our love, no financial worries, and a great sex life. Who needed more? Besides, I respected him for his abilities, and I was certain of his commitment and fidelity. I loved him! I surely wanted to live with him. I would have to take care of what I called "my social needs" myself.

Corinne now lived out of town, but I had Velma to listen to my troubles. Each in her own house, we had ten a.m. telephone breaks. I sat on the floor talking with Velma; next to me, Cathy sat, her little legs straight out in front of her, her delicate fingers twirling the dial on her toy telephone as she carried on animated conversations with a pretend friend. I listened to Velma's discontent, she to mine. Laughter at ourselves and each other helped.

Another source of support came from my sister. Ruth and Tryg moved to Minneapolis while Ruth and I were both pregnant with our second children. Living within walking distance of each other, we walked our babies together, shared lunches, and enjoyed each other. And on Wednesdays, Mary Donef, came into our house so I had a day off. Ruth brought Roxy over, and, leaving the two little girls in Mary's capable hands, we headed downtown. We shopped, tried on shoes, compared prices of lamp shades and bath towels, and had lunch in Dayton's fourth floor Tearoom. We talked and reminisced and dreamed of "someday." The adventure ended with a waltz through the aisles of Woolworth's— buttons to match one lost, nail polish remover, and, most important, presents for Cathy and Roxy. Then we went home.

With what gladness our girls greeted us upon our home-coming! Ours was just as great. Oh, it was a privilege to be home with our children when they were little. Cathy's baby arms around my neck, her warm, soft cheek next to mine, the smell of her hair, and the way she looked with one tear hanging on the lower lid, ready to fall. Sweet nostalgia!

Those were good days. I learned to see my marriage, not as perfect, perhaps, but better than average.

17.

Bruce Avenue

I sit at a typewriter in the southeast corner room of the second floor of the house in which I have lived with Paul for forty-five years. When we moved into 4516 Bruce Avenue in Edina, one month before our second daughter, Jane, was born, this space was the master bedroom. Following a 1955 remodeling job, Cathy owned the space, and, after Cathy's marriage, Jane moved in. Not ghosts, but Mucke family histories frolic about with my typewriter, desk, files and the bookshelves that hold authors "S" through "Z." Collages of friends and colleagues—pictures, maps, and mementoes of foreign travel—and needlework Paul stitched especially for me line walls and shelves. This is My Room of My Own.

We bought this house in 1944 for $8,950. It was an older home then, built in 1921. (I was seven years old.) Yet it stands proudly atop a small hill in the middle of the block, facing east; its French windows welcome the morning sun. The exterior is stucco, and the rooms converge on a center hall— all balanced and symmetrical. I find the thought of dying easier to face than giving up this space and cleaning out the basement.

*   *   *

Paul and I were pretty excited the day we moved in—he at forty and I at twenty-nine were homeowners! I sat on the sloping front lawn in a brown and white, checkered maternity dress. The style had not changed in the three years since I carried Cathy—same old butcher-boy style. With my protruding belly, I was in charge of Cathy, while Gramma Mucke washed woodwork inside and Paul directed the moving operation. A neighbor, Lucille Johnson, holding the hands of her twins, Gerry and Joanne, came to talk with us. The twins were just Cathy's age, would be her playmates and school friends for the next sixteen years. That first visit with Lucy blossomed into a friendship strong even now.

Jane was born three days before my thirtieth birthday. Lying in the hospital after her birth, I cried all day . . . I don't know why new mothers do that sometimes. By the time we brought Jane home, my world was shining. Soon after, the whole world was shining and optimistic—the war had ended. The Muckes were a typical suburban family with two children and I felt privileged to stay home.

I enjoyed baking on Saturdays, cleaning and moving furniture about on Fridays, laundry on Mondays—until we bought an automatic washer. I diapered Jane, toilet trained Cathy, opened millions of cans of Campbell's chicken soup (with noodles) and tuna fish, dropped endless teaspoons of chocolate chip cookie dough onto shiny aluminum sheets. I baked my own bread and declared to all who would listen that if more women stood with open windows on an early summer morning and allowed themselves the joy of kneading bread, the world would be a better place.

I planned my menus for the week. Milk was delivered to our back door in glass bottles, and the groceries and meats I ordered over the phone from the Morningside Grocery were delivered to my kitchen counter. I over-fed Jane, who ate Pablum as long as I spooned it in, and invented games to get Cathy to finish her green beans. By the time Paul arrived home at five thirty, I was cleaned up, the house orderly and the children clean and rested. At six o'clock, I served a properly balanced meal at the dining room table—place mats, goblets, and centerpiece—and encouraged "discussion" on our day.

Nobody pretended that caring for small children twenty-four hours a day was or is an easy task. Cathy and Jane's peak energy periods did not always correlate with mine. Their use of the word "No!" tried my patience; their tears and screams tried my nerves. Once, only once, I spanked Cathy with a hairbrush and still carry the guilt. But, oh, I did enjoy them.

Many mothers were home in that era, and I had plenty of company—tea parties with children and mothers, swimming, and picnics at the beach. Ruth's second daughter was born three weeks after Jane. Ruth and I and our four small children spent many hours together. Our cousins Big Edith and Helen, living in St. Louis Park, both had children the ages of Roxy and Cathy, and we also spent time together. I have many happy memories of walking or driving "to the corner" with Cathy and Jane—to Carlson's Odd Shop for a birthday present or to Joyce's Bakery for treats or to the library for books to be read at night and looked at during naps.

I took Cathy and Jane to Sunday School, continued to read my Christian Science lesson daily and, when I had time to think about it, found life good.

I took my child-rearing responsibilities seriously. During those years, psychologists and doctors reminded mothers that it was all up to them—the future of children was in their hands. I had been raised to believe (and did believe) that my life was my responsibility. If things went wrong, it was my own fault. Now I was told (and never questioned) that if things went wrong for Cathy and Jane, it was also my fault; if they "turned out well," Paul's and my good parenting was largely responsible. Years later, it occurred to me that I had assumed the responsibility (and guilt!) for two generations—and that seemed hardly fair.

* * *

The girls grew, and we prospered—a nuclear family with two children, a fine green lawn with pine trees and two cars in the garage. No accidents and no serious illnesses.

Soon both girls were in school, and, although they

walked home from Wooddale School for lunch while they watched Casey Jones on TV, I had more freedom. I could shop without children at Lund's Grocery Store, visit or have coffee with Lucy, read for an uninterrupted hour. The house was mine for several hours a day.

On a rainy September morning in 1946, the year before Roxy and Cathy started school, Ruth and Tryg moved to Sioux City. I missed them dearly and cried realizing I would not see Roxy and Mary grow up with Cathy and Jane. But, oh, it was a good day that spring morning in 1948 when Mother called me long distance (in the middle of the morning) to say that Papa had sold the store. They moved to a house (a real house with a basement and a porch and upstairs and downstairs) half a block from the shores of Lake Harriet near the park where Cathy and Jane played in summer and I took them sliding in winter.

High points of those years were our Florida vacations. From 1947 through 1959, we spent three weeks each spring on the west coast of Florida. Automobile trips the first years were great adventures. Paul was a skilled driver and map reader and a patient father; all I had to do was keep the children happy and quiet in the car. We stopped to buy new coloring books in dime stores and found swings in parks. We played in village squares and ate chocolate ice cream in drug stores with marble counters.

Crossing a state line was an event. In Tennessee, Cathy looked worried and seriously announced, "I've looked and watched and watched, and none of the kids I see are wearing tennis shoes."

We picked cotton in a hot, grey-white field and, with permission, oranges in a shady grove. And when we hung over a bridge over the Suwannee River, Cathy ordered Jane, "Watch for the swans!" We stopped early enough each afternoon to swim in a motel pool or take a walk and dined each evening on lobster, steak or lamb chops. Father was generous: no restrictions when the girls studied the menu.

What wonderful places the 1940 Florida Gulf beaches were for children. We all swam and played on the white sand, collected shells to dry and identify and carry home to our basement. We read books during nap time, played four-handed card games and went out to dinner each evening. It was a fine holiday from housework for me.

*   *   *

Paul continued his Shrine activities. The girls were excited and proud to see their Daddy march in parades, and we had the best seats at the annual Shrine Circus where Daddy sold peanuts.

Both girls swam competitively. Paul became president of the Minnesota Amateur Athletic Union, and for years the whole family spent summer weekends at swimming meets. All four of us swam in "Down the Mississippi" marathons at the Minneapolis Athletic Club, bringing home trophies for shelves and, eventually, our basement. We all bowled— Paul and I each in singles leagues and the two of us in a mixed league one night a week. Family bowling often followed Sunday dinners at the Club.

The girls outgrew babysitters. One of the first nights we left them alone, I was called to the phone at the bowling alley. I listened to Cathy's near-hysterical voice saying, "Mother! Jane has a bad side ache, and she's crying." I was well aware of Jane's crying in the background. I was panic stricken driving home. "Be careful. Be careful," I told myself. "I won't help Jane or Cathy if I have an accident. Be careful! What a long way home. What a long way home. What if . . ."

At home I found the two of them sitting calmly in our big bed. They had been reading *Little Women*; Beth's death had caused Jane's tears. The side ache had vanished.

*   *   *

I remember when Cathy and Jane and their friends came home from school in the afternoon. There was always food. Sometimes we had happy talks, sometimes arguments; often we had extracurricular activities. After they had completed the required driving school lessons, I spent hours driving beside them. Junior and senior high years: Do we let them do this? When do we say yes? When no? Will they be home on time? Is that boy a good driver? Those difficult memories are less pleasant, but time brings perspective and smiles.

Once, long after Cathy was married and had almost finished raising her two sons, I called her on a Halloween evening.

"Oh, Mother," Cathy said, "Marc, with his new driving license, is out tonight with the car for the very first time alone. Here it is Halloween, and I think of all those little ghosts running about in their white sheets and the devils in their little black costumes, and it's raining, and all those slippery leaves on the street, and Marc driving alone for the first time. Oh, Mother! Do you know how hard it is to be a mother?"

I know. But I think of those children coming in the front door after school, or after a prom, or a satisfying date, and I feel good all over.

When I was forty-four, Cathy graduated from high school and entered the University of Minnesota. A year later she was married, and Jane was making plans to leave home for Duke University. I had spent a lot of time with Cathy and Jane and their friends. When the moon was full and I couldn't sleep, I wondered how I would face the loneliness that stretched ahead. My lashes grew wet, tears rolled down the sides of my face into my ears. Not wanting to disturb my sleeping husband, I stifled sobs. But I was scared.

I listened to Jack Ludwig's University of Minnesota humanities lecture on the television, began to read Freud, and responded to a small newspaper item describing a new program at the university. The Minnesota Plan for Continuing Education for Women changed my life.

Part VI

18.

Cap and Gown

Cap and Gown Day. Wearing a black graduation gown and mortar board, I belong, am part of all this pomp and ceremony. My knees shake, and my throat is dry. I'm nervous as a bride, far more nervous than when I walked to the marriage altar. A bride. Yes. Of course. A love affair. And now I'm taking unto me this university . . . to love and to cherish . . . to support and uphold . . .

Love affair. That's what I have been having these past years, a great love affair with the University of Minnesota. Sunshine and blue skies glorify the mall this Wednesday morning, but in rain, wind—I remember the fall quarter I crossed the bridge every day, feeling like Mary Poppins, who might go up with her umbrella any moment—and Minnesota snow, I have loved this campus. Loved libraries and the classrooms, teachers and students, even the blue books.

What makes this day so special for each of us about to march down this mall? Going to class was always (well, almost always) an unqualified pleasure for me. Everyone of us here knows intimately the hours of pre-exam study, the tensions and sometimes fear. And all of the papers all of us researched, rough drafted, tore up, re-roughed, wrote, rewrote and typed!

A love affair. Sentimentality. It's supposed to be out of date, but I am crying. I must not cry because, when salt collects on the edges of my contact lenses, it hurts.

*   *   *

Those good years began one 1961 November day—not just "one" November day. November 7, 1961. I celebrate its anniversary. A dark, dirty, dreary November day. I started the day bowling in my Ladies League and taking a recently widowed friend to lunch. Pleasant but enervating pasttimes. I had a two o'clock appointment with Dr. Vera Schletzer, counselor with the university's Minnesota Plan for Continuing Education for Women. I arrived at the campus with plenty of time, or so I thought, to park my car and find my way to Eddy Hall.

Thirty or forty minutes later, while my now uncomfortable heels dug into the eighth or tenth block of hard campus sidewalk and my contact-lensed eyes felt as though they were being lanced by many needles, I muttered sad phrases to myself, questioning my sanity. I had a new grandson; I should be satisfied to visit and rock the dear little boy. After all, what was wrong with staying home and baking excellent sugar cookies?

A particularly vicious gust of wind tore my good black hat (we all wore smart ladies' hats in 1961) from my head. After chasing it, in the direction opposite to the flow of students, down the middle of the street for half a block or more, I recovered the hat but lost my self-confidence. I began to doubt my adjustment to life. Miraculously, I did not return to my car. Though late, I followed through with my appointment.

An hour or more later, I left all my doubts and fifteen years of wear and tear in Dr. Schletzer's office. She found me a likely candidate for a special liberal arts seminar and suggested I make application for New Worlds of Knowledge. While I waited to be accepted, she suggested that I take a correspondence course. She did not see me as a grandmother, or, if she did, she did not let me know. Leaving her office, my shoes felt like tennis shoes. The bounce and spring in my whole body reflected the great sense of well-being. The greatest!

The correspondence course suggested by the wise counselor (now my good friend Vera) was an exciting beginning. How I devoured that pyschology text! Dr. Dorothy Bird's encouragement and inspiration reinforced my enthusiasm. I practically memorized the text and earned the highest grade ever given a student in the course. Talk about overachieving.

My success with the psych class and acceptance as a student in the New Worlds of Knowledge seminar gave Schletzer's suggestion that I work toward a degree some credibility. My freshman credits (1931-1932) were good. Why not go for it—make a start? That year I spent with the students and professors in that seminar taught me that Freud was correct when he suggested that there is no pleasure in life compared with the joy of intellectual stimulation. If I had not been starving for that, I certainly had been on a lean diet. I was in every sense the woman described in Betty Friedan's *The Feminine Mystique*: wife, mother, community activist, club woman.

"But, Dr. Schletzer," I said, "if I don't go full-time, and I can't imagine that I would, I'll be over fifty years old when I graduate in '66 or '67."

"In 1966 or 1967, you'll be over fifty whether you graduate or not," replied the good counselor. "Take your choice: fifty with or without a degree."

The daughters Paul and I had raised (following all the rules, formulas, and advice of my doctor and *McCall's* magazine) were growing up; Cathy was married, and Jane was about to graduate, making plans to leave for college. Viewed at first with tolerance and some amusement, Paul thought the plan "an okay thing to do." Originally I planned my schedule so that I left home after Paul did and arrived home before him, but his support was whole-hearted and loving; he often left home earlier than necessary to drive me to classes.

That summer, my collegiate daughter from Duke suggested we take a summer school class together. What fun! I was a serious degree candidate, and I had a parking space

that summer. Innocently, I had walked into the Police Department and asked for a space—and they gave it to me. It
must have been a mistake. Dr. Schletzer said, "PhDs are a
dime a dozen on this campus, but the people who really count
are those with parking spaces."

Jane and I sat together in English Literature. Despite
gaps in my knowledge, evident to me not only by Dr. Unger's
references but by remarks made by the many graduate students in the class, I had my moments. Like when Dr. Unger
said, in explaining a John Donne poem, "There used to be a
song called 'Did You Ever See a Dream Walking?' and that's
what this poem's saying. But, of course, *you* are all too young
to remember that." Then he looked at me and smiled.

I also took a course in physical anthropology. A freshman level course and taken by many teachers, but I was
scared. Could I learn the stuff? Paripethecus and propli-
apithecus in Egypt. Proconsul in Africa. More. Would I ever
be able to spell them, let alone remember who they were?
When the midquarter exams came back, I had earned a big
fat D. My children laughed. I did not see the humor. They
said, "This may not indicate what you learned in anthropology, but you sure learned a lesson in humility, and you
probably needed that."

Jane did all her studying while riding back and forth to
school with me driving; she spent afternoons and evenings
playing and swimming in the Aqua Follies. I studied all after-
noon and often late into the night. She earned three A's—in
English Literature, Macro Economics, and Micro Economics.
I earned a B in the English course and a C in Anthropology.
The only C on my transcript, it remains the grade in which
I take the most pride.

*   *   *

The steps leading to the overbridge were icy in winter.
Walking across campus, everyone seemed to truly "suffer"
the winds. It became a matter of sheer physical survival—life
on the Minnesota campus in the winter. I asked myself why I
didn't mind the physical discomfort. Why did I enjoy the
climb? Neitzsche's Zarathustra said, "Life wants to build it-

self up into the heights with pillars and steps; it wants to look into vast distances and out toward stirring beauties; therefore, it requires heights. And because it requires height, it requires steps and contradiction among the steps and the climbers. Life wants to climb and to overcome itself climbing."

Not all the walks over the bridge to the West Bank were icy or hard. Once I walked with a young married woman from India. She said she would return to India and tell her people that in the United States very old ladies went to college. A young male friend in a philosophy class often took me to Newman Center for coffee. He said, "Oh, I wish my mother understood me the way you do. I wish I could talk to her the way I talk to you." When I told this to Paul, he laughed and said it was better than my sitting over cocktails downtown and having some man say he wished *his wife* understood him as well as I did.

I had friends the ages of my own two daughters, yet I thought of these people as contemporaries. I didn't feel any older than they. We shared concerns, ideas, and library problems. I was always surprised when I caught a glimpse of myself in a mirror; I had begun to think of myself as looking more like my friends.

It was not unusual to have young men and women say to me, "I think you're wonderful. I wish *my* mother would do this." Then one day one curly-haired, black-eyed young woman said to me, "It's so neat to have somebody your age here on campus. I wish my *grandmother* would do this!"

It all passed so quickly. The quarters and years didn't slip by, they tore by. The credits piled up; even though I dragged it out, I finally had only one class left to take to graduate—Public Health 2. I squeaked by with a B and graduated with the 1967 class, being awarded a degree cum laude.

A love affair with those halls of learning.

Jane came from Florida, Cathy brought her children, and Paul was there. The band played. The graduating class marched up the steps into Northrup Memorial Auditorium:

FOUNDED IN THE FAITH THAT MEN ARE
ENNOBLED BY UNDERSTANDING
DEDICATED TO THE ADVANCEMENT OF LEARNING
AND THE SEARCH FOR TRUTH — DEVOTED TO
THE INSTRUCTION OF YOUTH AND
THE WELFARE OF THE STATE.

*   *   *

The band is playing louder. Why, that girl over there is wiping her eyes. She's only eighteen or twenty. Sentimentality may be out of date, but good honest emotion is not. But, I must not cry . . . these contacts . . .

19.

Continuing Education
for Women

"But, Edith, if you're going to graduate school, and if you're going to do anything on campus, shouldn't it be with us, here at Continuing Education for Women?"

Such was the response of Louise Roff, director of CEW, when I told her that Professor Ames had suggested I might have an assistantship in the Humanities Department if I considered graduate school. But the flexibility of administration fit my schedule better than teaching, and Louise cleared the way for me to work part-time in the Extension Division, that unit of the university whose mission was the extension of its many resources to the community at large. What a fine solution for me; no need to face the decision of what to do with the rest of my life. I would not have to give up my good life on campus.

CEW was a small program—Louise, a secretary and me. I had a desk and a telephone and shared a room with two others in Nolte Center. I typed letters, answered phones, designed brochures, planned courses, talked with professors and monitored classes. I kept a time card and, twice a month, was paid $3.50 for the hours I had worked. Imagine being paid for something I would have done for nothing. This money was gravy—something I could do without, but it was delicious! Enthusiastic and energetic, working closely with Louise, I was never happier.

At the same time, I attended classes and wrote papers toward a master's degree in American Studies, enjoyed the intellectual stimulation and new friendships. But all that new learning did a pretty job of scrambling my thinking. Following my mother's death, I had left the Christian Science Church. It was not easy to relinquish my faith in that religion's teachings. Christian Science not only comforted my mother, but had comforted me to see how happy and secure she had been in her faith. After Ruth and I had left home, I knew her religion eased her loneliness and fear. I had never doubted that she had the right answers. None of us had ever gone to a doctor. We never had childhood diseases (well, except mumps), not even measles even though I slept with Cousin Edith when she had it.

But my mother died of breast cancer. Christian Science failed her. My metaphysical and philosophical underpinnings were seriously challenged. How could I, after spending hours with Alyosha and the Grand Inquisitor, accept God's infinite goodness to the exclusion and denial of what Mrs. Eddy and my mother called "error"? How could I spend time with Ilynsky, Dostoyevsky's Underground Man, and believe in the power of Reason, denying emotions. Lack of ritual and emotion in the Christian Science sermons had been explained to me as right and good because emotional influences were not to be trusted. To my great amusement, in reading *War and Peace*, I learned that Tolstoy felt opera was not to be trusted because the music attacked the emotions, playing havoc with reason.

When I came to Thomas Mann's *Magic Mountain*, I listened and watched Hans Castorp with Settembrini and Claudia, the polarities I saw to be the essence of whatever we tried to name "Truth," and I saw the wisdom of balance, compromise, the Golden Mean. What infinite arrogance for any person to *know* what's true! Or what was right for another. What arrogance, what hubris, I had been exhibiting for most of my young—now old—life!

Living through the turbulent sixties, I lost faith, as did

many, in the American Dream. I read James Agee and looked at photographs of the poor in the South. America's "Manifest Destiny" may not have been something ordained.

And yet, to become aware of all the questions and the doubt did not depress me. I became aware of a new sense of freedom as I walked with Camus and Emily Dickinson. The Existentialists were a relief. No need to deny what the material senses told me. I might continue to ask questions. But no need to understand. I didn't have to understand existence. I was. That was enough.

*   *   *

I was ready to work in Continuing Education for Women, the program that had changed my life. I talked with women, shared their triumphs and their despairs. I, too, knew the confusion and apprehension of not quite knowing how to register and the frustration of standing in lines. I could share with them the anxiety—the butterflies in the stomach and wet palms—before exams and before papers were returned. I understood their isolation in the classroom, competing with eighteen-year-olds. I knew what they meant when they said, "Old friends don't understand why I can't have lunch because I'm writing a paper." I laughed with them when we remembered what a chore Christmas used to be. "Now, if I can just get these damn papers written, shopping and Christmas cookies will be a snap." And I understood the guilt they suffered when husbands or family members acted neglected.

Concomitant with my growth, the program grew. Louise and I participated in panels on continuing education and talked to community groups about CEW classes and programs. Women flocked to a class Dr. Schletzer taught—Guidelines—that helped women answer the question: "What do I do with the rest of my life?" The women's movement and its branches were in full bloom.

CEW was originally established to serve college-educated women, but the lack of humanpower in the work force and the waste of women's abilities were of concern even before *The Feminine Mystique* was published. At the same time, women were becoming dissatisfied with their lives. The impact of the women's movement caused growth in CEW.

When I was awarded a master's degree, Continuing Education and Extension provided the financial support to hire me full-time on an academic appointment. There were four of us full-time in the department—a programmer, a secretary, Louise and me. By the fall of 1980, our staff numbered ten people.

Completely committed, I enjoyed planning programs that would do for other women what university classes and professors had done for me. I met with faculty staff and other educators who had plenty of good ideas and liked trying them out on mature women who would argue and question. I talked and listened to the women themselves. Heard excitement and joy in learning, stories of success when amassed credits resulted in graduations, how kids' grades improved with Mom's interest in education. Some women found exciting jobs; some graduated and taught.

There were sad stories too. Women who had slaved at typewriters or behind counters while husbands finished college, only to be left behind intellectually, often physically. Women in their fifties who had spent years with kids and house found themselves—through death or divorce—without real work or financial independence. Young women on AFDC unable to make it. Lack of self-esteem. Problems, problems, problems . . .

When Paul retired in 1968, neither of us talked about my leaving the university. We had an interesting and successful reversal of roles. Although our financial situation did not make it necessary for me to work, inflation and the amount of my salary checks had changed the nature of those dollars. My salary was no longer gravy, and I had acquired a taste for travel that Paul encouraged. He enjoyed cooking and polished his culinary skills (even took a cooking course offered through CEW) and gradually took on more of the housekeeping chores, rounding out his life with volunteer committee work for the Village of Edina and needlepoint. He enjoyed having the house to himself.

In 1972 I was appointed Assistant Professor on the tenure track. Louise Roff got ready to retire. Rules and regulations proliferated; although I had practically grown up with the Department and had served over four years as Assistant Director, a search committee was appointed to look for a new director. Though I had my ambivalences, I applied for the position. Application, interviews, and the final examination with the committee was an experience that called for every bit of courage and self-esteem I could pull together. But on that happy day when I learned that the position was mine, the staff poured champagne.

*   *   *

The years as Director were years of hard work, frustration, success and joy. Budget squeezes, occasional personnel problems and report deadlines cost me sleep, maybe, but my enthusiasm for the program never waned. Not to mention the self-esteem and fulfillment I felt being paid in cold hard cash and work that had meaning. My social needs were being met. Horizons, wrote Edna St. Vincent Millay, are as wide as the heart. I don't know what my mental limits are, but I watched my mental horizons widen and my spiritual horizons soar.

To remember that period, the third quarter of my life, is to think of many people. People always count the most for me. I think of counselors—not just Vera with her words that pushed me forward—but the personal concern and interest in me that Harold Miller, Don Woods, Sis Fenton, and Barbara Stuhler had, their belief in me. I think of the faculty and how I came to understand that my presence in the classes was important to me . . . and to the class. Roy Swanson, Oya Kaynor, Sarah Youngblood. I remember John Berryman's wit and encouragement, Mary Turpie's constant encouragement and friendliness, her pride in me. And the students . . . I remember them.

I was sixty-nine years old in June 1983 when I graduated from my work on campus. The way I felt about retirement is still evident in my reluctance to use the word "retire." I faced this stage of my life (the last quarter) of the past twenty years, fearing the lack of structure, fearing the loss of the social and intellectual companionship that was an

Edith, age sixty-five.

integral part of my daily life, yet sensing that this was the right time to leave—a year before retirement would be forced upon me.

How would I face this transition? Would the long list of things I had been planning and hoping to do in that distant future look as intriguing and fascinating as it looked earlier? Or would I give in to gravity and inertia and put comfort and lack of stress at the top of my list?

20.

I Stand Here Ironing

"I stand here ironing . . ."

Tillie Olsen has no corner on deep thinking while standing over an ironing board.

I have always liked to iron, work that results in a finished product. Mostly linen napkins. I iron the linen napkins from my mother's house.

Before they were married, my father sent my mother $800 from Sweden, told her to stop working, buy a sewing machine and work on linens for her hope chest. My mother's hands pushed and pulled a shining steel needle and white thread through this linen, rolling the hems of these fine napkins, over which my iron slides smoothly. "First on the right side," my mother taught me, "and then on the wrong side to bring out the embroidery and the texture of the linen."

I see her standing in the middle of our large white kitchen with the green and white linoleum block floor. The iron's cord, hung from the ceiling light fixture, sways with the movement of her arms. She wears a blue-and-white checkered Princess Peggy, rickrack-trimmed housedress that zips down the front. Her tan lisle stockings are thick enough to hide the varicose veins. Her black shoes with the sturdy Cuban heels are wide to make room for the large joints of her big toes. Her face is framed by the sculptured waves of dark brown bobbed and permed hair. Over her sad brown eyes, the bushy eyebrows—so like her father's—go up and down as we talk.

How I loved coming home from school on Tuesday—the day after wash day, the day Mother ironed. I see myself, a skinny, long-legged child of ten, walking into the white kitchen made lighter by the afternoon sunshine streaming in the two west windows. A white enameled table. An embroidered cloth (muslin ironed to look like linen), a flower garden of lazy daisy, outline and running stitches and French knots. The two rectangular Pyrex pans of cinnamon rolls, fresh from the oven. And my mother ironing. I rush to the bathroom, then drop my school books on my desk and return to the kitchen. Hooking my heels over the front rung of a white kitchen chair with the curved back, I face Mother at her ironing board.

Cinnamon roll in hand (or an icebox cookie with crescent teeth marks), I plead with her, "Mother, can't I please stop taking music lessons? I'm so tired of practicing, and I hate it so much! There are better things for me to do!"

"Certainly not," she replies, ignoring my plea, "and how did Miss Jensen like the corrected map of South America? Did she think it looked less like an ice cream cone?"

"Do you think I'm really smart, Mother? Today when Miss Jensen read about a lady who swept the floor and no dust went before her broom, she asked us what that meant. Nobody else in the class raised her hand except me."

"What did it mean?" Mother smiles.

"It means that the lady's floor was awfully clean. Honestly, Agatha Swanson is really *dumb*."

"You must not call people dumb, Edith. You use that word too much, and Papa was talking to you about that last night at supper."

She introduces another subject. She and Papa have talked it over, and she is not going to sew winter coats for Ruth and me this year. They have decided that they will drive us to Estherville, Iowa, where we will buy coats at Martins' Merchandising Mart. Store-bought coats! Yes, maybe I can have a coat with a fur collar.

The napkin satin smooth and stiff as a board, her gnarled hands slide over it, gently, oh, so gently folding it— over once, and over once more. Large and stiff with the satin stitch embroidered initial "J" standing upright in the corner, the napkin is ready for guests.

My mother smiles. But her eyes speak of a deep melancholy. Why do I think of her eyes as sad brown eyes? Because something about those eyes betrayed a knowledge of pain, of life's difficulties. Life is difficult. There is no easy way to live it. But that great truth admitted, my mother transcends it. There is room for joy and laughter. We are strong Viking women. Survivors. All of this I read in my mother's eyes. "The rain may fall on us," she said, "but we do not melt."

"What a beautiful day!" So she greeted every day. Rain or shine, snow or sleet, the weather and temperature were always just right for some particular task or event. And so today Ruth and I laugh when our friends tell us we are absolutely obnoxious in our good humor about the weather. Every morning we find beautiful. "This," our mother explained, "is the day that the Lord hath made. Be glad, give thanks, rejoice!" And she did.

*   *   *

Ironing. A refuge, an activity night or day that quenches the flow of whatever it is that causes nervous legs and restlessness. I have never been a really good sleeper. When the girls were young and I did all the laundry and those sleepless white nights came upon me, nights when the full moon stole sleep from me, I would sneak quietly down two flights of stairs to the basement where the Peter Pan round-collared blouses, the Ship-and-Shore tailored shirts and the green and red plaid or the pink broadcloth dresses, the white shirts without starch in the collars, waited to be ironed. I stood in the laundry, non-recreation-room basement, and ironed. Then I would creep quietly back upstairs for a sound sleep. When morning came, it was as though fairies had done my work while I slept.

A refuge, did I say? When in 1962, I found a lump the

size of a walnut in my breast, a lump that appeared as though by magic, the terror, the certainty that I would surely be dead in a short time, produced in me such a panic that I had no hope of sleeping. From one o'clock until three in the morning, tears streaming down my face and onto the cotton skirts and blouses that my high school senior Jane would wear, I prayed that I would be allowed to live to see my first-born grandson, Scott, grow—at least long enough to see him start school. For the first time, over my ironing board, I faced the truth of my own mortality.

The lump turned out to be a mass of something unimportant, nonmalignant.

*   *   *

Ironing and my mother. Mortality. Immortality. She never gave up easily nor expected Ruth and me to give up. Like her, we were good housekeepers. "You two girls," she said, "do your housework as though it should have been finished yesterday."

Ironing. I come from a long line of Viking women. We are survivors, we do not melt, and we do not give up. I *will* write about us . . .

*   *   *

These stiff white napkins I iron, these napkins my guests admired last evening, these napkins the ironing of which brings me such happy memories . . .

Who will iron these napkins when I die?

*   *   *

This book is finished. I am an old woman, many jobs and careers ended, but I still have work to do. People live now to the age of one hundred years, and I may have (in calendar time) a quarter of my life left. My work is not finished. Work, like connections, is an important word. A loaded word. My real work is not what I did for a pay check; my work is my response to the call of life—for isn't life itself a "calling"?

I like to think of my work as a celebration of the life given me, the creation of myself. Celebrate because life (just being alive) is something to celebrate. *Celebrate* because the very idea of celebration suggests people and joy. And life (LIFE) is with people. *Create* because out of that swarming and random combination of genes I was given, I accept the responsibility for the creation of Edith. That's my real work. My real work goes on—integrating, assimilating, sorting and loving. This will go on until I take my last breath. Maybe longer.

Meanwhile, I have a pair of white satin wedding shoes in my basement. . . .